THE JOY OF
CURLING

A CELEBRATION

First published in 1990 by
McGraw-Hill Ryerson Limited
330 Progress Avenue
Scarborough, Ontario M1P 2Z5

Produced for McGraw-Hill Ryerson Limited by Tormont
Publications Inc., Montreal, Canada

Editors: Angela Rahaniotis, Andrew Carter
Graphic Design and Layout: ZAPP
Front Jacket Design: Bodson, Gauthier et Associés.

ISBN 0-07-549951-7

Printed and bound in Canada

THE JOY OF
CURLING

A CELEBRATION

ED LUKOWICH
EIGIL RAMSFJELL
BUD SOMERVILLE

McGraw-Hill Ryerson

Toronto Montreal

The Curling Game

Detail from " The Curlers" by Sir George Harvey.

Here's to the sport of fair renown,
Here's to the roarin' game;
Here's to the stones that go gliding down,
Here's to the icy lane:
Here's to the skip with shout so bold,
Here's to his players' fling,
Here's to the game that is never old,
Here's to the songs we sing.

O curlers, come, we're brithers a',
Come join the curling game;
Our eyes are keen, our arms are true,
Our courage is aflame;
In winter air, and sport so rare,
The stones our weapons be,
We'll make the fight with honest might,
To gain the victory:
A man who is a curling man,
No better man than he.

*This book is a tribute
to a sport that has enriched our
lives, expanded our horizons
and brought us immense joy.*

*We invite you
to share the feeling.*

Ed, Eigil, Bud

Table of Contents

The Joy of Curling

I was six the first time I picked up a curling rock in the little town of Speers, Saskatchewan, (pop. 150).

Curling has inspired intense emotions in me for as long as I can remember. I played in the school bonspiel in grade one and when they raised the age requirement the next year, I was crushed and burst into tears.

I was always happiest on the ice, playing, practicing and striving to improve. My first delivery was a two-handed push with a belly-flop follow-through.

I immersed myself in the game. The book *Ken Watson on Curling* became my bible. I studied Watson's every technique, determined to emulate his famous slide.

I made the high school team in seventh grade, and went on to compete in the Canadian High School Championships. By grade nine our upstart little town was at the Nationals, and the following year my brother Mike skipped our team all the way to a Canadian title.

Though I played other sports, curling was always my first love. I got a charge out of the movement of the stones on impact, the universe of different shots, the flow of the delivery and the all-out sweeping effort.

As the stakes grew later on, so did the thrill. My heart soared and plummeted with the intense pressure of cash bonspiels and the Brier playdowns. To win the bursting pride and joy of going to the Brier was the highest glory, and on losing out, the wait until next year seemed an eternity.

Curling was life for me. The rest of the world ceased to exist inside the higher world of a big match.

But no matter where I travel, the intensity on the ice is matched by a goodwill off the ice, a shared refreshment, a couple of laughs and a fellowship that is unsurpassed. Those who have been swept up in its spell know that no other game can match curling in its sportsmanship and camaraderie. Thanks to curling I've made friends worldwide, and I wouldn't trade that for anything.

Ed visits the old condemned natural ice two-sheeter curling rink where his dad, Button Joe, the ice maker, introduced him to the sport.

I was in eighth grade in 1970 when my P.I. teacher Dag Tucker took my class to the Askerhallen, a recently-built curling and hockey arena near Oslo. We had been told to bring our most slippery dancing shoe for our left foot and a jogging shoe for our right. With this equipment, we were introduced to "the roaring game".

I was 15 and an ardent and promising soccer player and I was not looking forward to a long cold winter of indoor training. I was immediately captivated by the game and the challenge of the difficult mechanics thrilled me.

Dag Tucker organized a bonspiel as a final exam for the course. We lined up foursomes, each made up of two second-year curlers and two beginners.

Dag confessed later that he had introduced difficult, even potentially criminal students to the game in an effort to straighten them up. He also hadn't taught us much about the sportsmanship of curling. This resulted in our skip telling us, as he readied to shoot his last rock, to burn his stone upon a secret command that he was going to give us if it looked as though he would raise an opponent's stone in for shot rock. Fortunately, we didn't have to cheat and I completed my debut on a winning note.

There was no turning back after that. Our mothers had to hold many a supper on the stove for us as we stole onto the ice almost daily on our way home from school to spend hours throwing stones.

It wasn't long before my dedication paid off. My team made it to the final in Norway's first junior competition in March 1971, only to finish second to a team from Brumunddal skipped by my later teammate Kristian Soerum. No one dreamed that eight years later we would win the World final against local favorite Peter Attinger in Berne, Switzerland, in front of the largest single-game crowd to date.

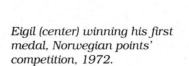

Eigil (center) winning his first medal, Norwegian points' competition, 1972.

Left to right, Jack Horst, Bud, Ray (Bud's dad), Bob Gradin: U.S. national team, 1962.

Curling has been a big part of my life for as far back as I can remember. As a youngster in Superior, Wisconsin, I loved going down to the local natural ice rink with Mom to watch Dad curl. I was about ten when I first took to the ice. During the more than 40 years since then, the game has brought me both joy and frustration.

I've met people from all over the world and have curled with and against some of the best, but what stands out is when I played with my father Ray and son Tim in U.S. national competition. We almost made it all the way, coming one game short, twice, from competing together in the World championship.

I have played other sports, but none have given me as much enjoyment as curling. In my mind, nothing competes with curling and I will continue to slide, sweep and deliver for as long as I can. But even if I'm not able to curl, the memories the game has blessed me with will remain with me the rest of my life.

The Origin
of Curling

The precise beginnings of curling are shrouded in history. It is not hard to imagine a man, hundreds or even thousands of years ago, weigh a smooth, heavy rock in his hand and then watch with fascination as he launched it as far as he could see along a glistening bed of ice. The grumbling roar a stone makes as it slides on ice has lent a nickname to curling; it is often referred to as "the roaring game".

Scots and continental Europeans have engaged in many a lively dispute as to the true origin of the game, both claiming to be the founders. Was curling brought to Scotland by Flemish sportsmen who emigrated during the reign of James VI (James I of England), or did Europeans always play some other form and the Scots really invented curling? The evidence, based on early stones, certain 16th century works of art and 17th century writings, has sparked a number of theories, but it remains inconclusive.

Some of the earliest records of a game similar to curling date from 1565. Two oil paintings by the Dutch master Pieter Bruegel, entitled "Winter Landscape with Skaters and a Birdtrap" and "Hunters in the Snow", show *eisschiessen* or "ice shooting", a Bavarian game played with a long stick-like handle, that is still enjoyed today.

Another work, an engraving by R. de Baudous (1575-1644) after N. van Wieringen, entitled "Hyems" or "Winter", shows players who appear to be sliding large discs of wood along a frozen waterway. Other records from around the same time show a hardy Dutch game called kuting, played with frozen lumps of earth.

The first reference to what could have been an early curling game dates from February 1540, when John McQuhin of Scotland recorded, in Latin, a challenge to a game on ice between a monk named John Sclater and an associate, Gavin Hamilton.

The word "curling" first appears in print in an elegy written in 1620 by Henry Adamson following the death of close friend James Gall, who was obviously a sporting gentleman. *His name was M. James Gall, a citizen of Perth, and a gentle-man of goodly stature, and pregnant wit, much given to pastime, as golf, archerie, curling and jovial companie.*

To add to the puzzle, a curling stone (the famous Stirling Stone) inscribed with the date 1511 turned up and another bearing the date 1551 was found when an old pond was drained at Dunblane, Scotland.

Detail from Pieter Bruegel's "Hunters in the Snow", 1565.

"Winter Landscape with Skaters and a Birdtrap", by Pieter Bruegel, 1565.

The controversy over the true birthplace of the game was initiated by the Reverend John Ramsay of Gladsmuir, Scotland. In his book, *An Account of the Game of Curling* (Edinburgh 1811), he argued in favor of Continental beginnings. His research into the origins of curling words (examples: bonspiel, brough, colly, curl, kuting, quoiting, rink, and wick), led him to conclude that they were derived from Dutch or German. Claiming that most of the words were foreign, he wrote, "but the whole of the terms being Continental compel us to ascribe to a Continental origin."

The famous historian, the Reverend John Kerr contested Ramsay's views and campaigned in favor of Scottish beginnings to curling in *A History of Curling* (1890). If the Flemings brought curling to Scotland in the 16th century, Kerr wondered why Scottish poets and historians made no mention of curling before 1600. He also saw no proof that many of the terms were Continental, explaining that many were of Celtic or Teutonic origin (examples: channel stone, crampit, draw, hack, hog, skip, tee, toesee, tramp, and tricker).

"It is absurd," he wrote, "that, if the game were Flemish and carried with Flemings wherever they settled, it would only be in Scotland that primitive stones would be found." A simple answer might be that the Flemings may have played with frozen clods of earth which later thawed, leaving no trace.

Curling was a familiar word in 17th-century Scotland. For example, records from a Glasgow Assembly of Presbyterians in 1638 accused a certain Bishop Graham of Orkney of a terrible act, "He was a curler on the ice on the Sabbath."

An early description of curling is found in a poem by James Graeme written in 1773.

The goals are marked out; the centre each
Of a large random circle; distance scores
Are drawn between, the dread of weakly arms
Firm on his cramp-bits stands the steady youth
Who leads the game: low o'er the weighty stone
He bends incumbent, and with nicest eye
Surveys the further goal, and in his mind
Measures the distance; careful to bestow
Just force enough; then, balanc'd in his hand
He flings it on direct; it glides along
Hoarse murmuring, while, plying hard before,
Full many a besom sweeps away the snow
Or icicle, that might obstruct its course....

"Hyems" ("Winter"), engraving by
R. de Baudous after a painting by
N. van Wieringen.

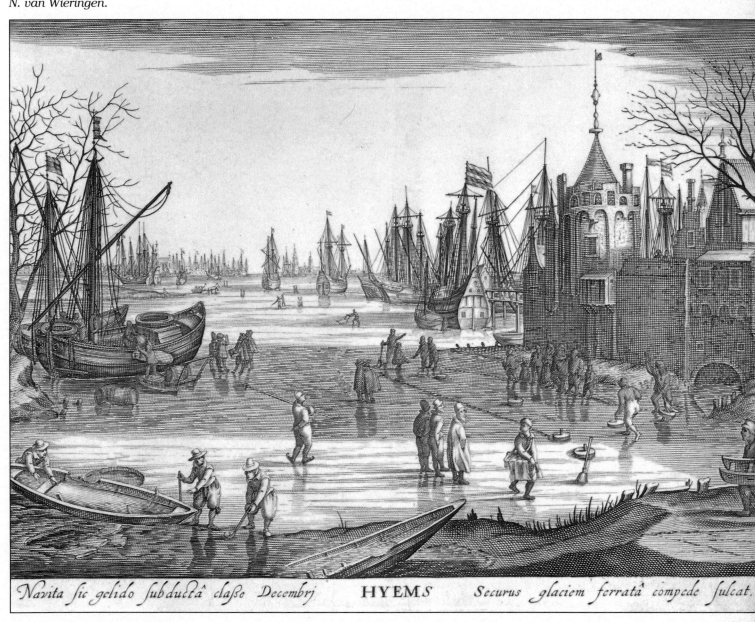

Navita fic gelido fubductâ claſſe Decembrj HYEMS *Securus glaciem ferratâ compede fulcat.*

The game of "eisschiessen", or "ice shooting" as played in Bavaria (left) and Austria (below).

There are several references to curling as a common practice in Scotland between 1700 and 1800. We read about bonspiels, curling societies being formed, and curling is referred to as a great national game.

The true origin of curling is cloudy, lost in the mists of time. There is no doubt or dispute, however, that the Scots nurtured the game, improved it, established rules, turned it into a national pastime and exported it to many other countries.

Stones

Curling stones have changed dramatically from the first recorded kuting stones of the 16th century. Pioneer curlers graduated to rough boulders with handles around 1650, then rounded stones, which evolved into the precision stones with cupped running surfaces and moulded plastic handles used today.

Kuting stones (1500-1650) varied in weight from five to 25 pounds. There were indents chiselled for the thumb and finger to allow a better grip. The most famous kuting stone was a 26-pounder, called the Stirling Stone, which has 1511 etched on one side. Early kuting stones were called channel-stones because they were picked up from riverbeds where they had worn smooth. It took plenty of strength to grasp and throw these early stones, which probably meant that not too many women or children participated.

The curling stone evolved from the early kuting stone (front, center) to the handle stone (back, left) to the rounded stone (front, right) to the iron (front, left) to the modern stone (back, center and right).

It wasn't until 1650 that someone attached a handle to the stone to make it easier to control the heavier stones and improve on the accuracy of players. With the arrival of the handle, rocks increased in size, and became something of a status symbol, as the strongest men equipped themselves with their own personal rocks.

The largest "boss" stone on display is the "Jubilee", which weighs in at an intimidating 117 pounds. The delivery of one of these giants often cleared the rink, as players and spectators dove for cover to avoid flying chips.

Before the advent of round stones, curlers owned and sized their own stones. Without standards,

stones were known to have rough edges, square spots, and were of varying weights and sizes. This allowed no uniformity of play. Heavier stones dominated if ice conditions were keen and fast. Damp and slow ice made it easier to fling the light stones the length of the sheet to win.

By 1825, round stones were the ones most commonly used. They rebounded more consistently bringing more skill to the game and making for better shots.

Painstaking experimentation by J.S. Turner of Toronto resulted in the development, in 1879, of a stone suited to all ice conditions. Andrew Kay of Ayrshire, Scotland applied Turner's specifications and began to machine-tool curling stones. This was the dawn of matched sets and equal weights.

A later improvement was the concave cup with a thin round edge on the bottom of the stone to lessen friction on the ice. By varying the depth and diameter of the cup, the stone maker designed the bottom of the stone with a sharp side, and the top with a dull side, to be turned over depending on ice conditions. A seven-inch sole was used for keen ice, and a three-inch base for slow ice.

Uniform striking bands completed the improvement, allowing stones of the same weight, height, circumference, running edge and size of handle to be manufactured. Clubs soon opted to own matched sets of stones, and eventually, due to the consistency of indoor ice, top and bottom cups were made the same, making curling an equal opportunity sport.

From the 16th century to the first half of the 20th century, the tiny Scottish island of Ailsa Craig provided the granite for curling stones. But quarrying at Ailsa Craig was uneconomical, and in 1946, stone masons Charles and Robert Wyllie found a new source of quality granite on the sea cliffs of Trevor in North Wales. Two companies compete in the business of making granite rocks, one in Mauchline, Scotland, and the other in North Wales.

The concave cup on the bottom of the stone forms the running surface.

The standard curling stone weighs between 42 and 44 pounds, a great deal more compact than some of the early monsters, but still too heavy for children.

The last few years have seen the introduction of 25-lb. stones for youngsters, made of granite, but ground smaller. There are also Jam Pail plastic stones that can be varied in weight for different strengths and 17-lb. plastic "stones" that are catching on like wildfire. The lighter stones make curling more fun and easier for junior curlers to learn.

*Far left: wicker basket
for stone
Center: irons
Right: early granite
stones*

An interesting footnote to the history of the curling stone is the use of the curling iron, which was almost exclusive to the province of Quebec, Canada until the 1950s.

After the fall of Quebec City to the British in 1759, men of the 78th Highlanders were looking for leisure activities. With a shortage of available granite, they received permission to melt down cannon balls to use for curling on the St. Charles River.

Curlers used 45-lb. to 65-lb. irons at Canada's first curling club, the Royal Montreal Curling Club, founded in 1807.

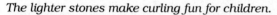

The lighter stones make curling fun for children.

Brushes,
Brooms

The evolution of sweeping and different types of brooms was the result of curlers in Scotland, Europe and later North America, crossing paths.

When Scots began curling, they used the kowe, similar to an old wisp, to clear snow from the path of the speeding stone. By 1850 some curlers had switched to wide house-type straw brooms. Early immigrants to Canada preferred the kitchen broom.

Exactly when Scots first used the push broom is not clearly recorded. By 1920 some Scots were trying push brooms made of hair, or brushes, until they eventually became the favorite curling tool, as they are today.

Continental Europe's sweeping choices copied both Scotland and Canada.

Between 1850 and 1960, wide straw booms gave way to the almost exclusive use of brushes. This changed when Canadians began traveling to Europe to teach curling from the 1960s to 1980. During this time the corn broom, and some artificial variations like the "rink rat", were in almost 100% use in Canada. Canadian teachers persuaded some European curlers to adopt the modern corn broom, a sleeker, more efficient form of the old wide house broom. Today European curlers lean about 90%-10% in favor of the brush.

Canadian curlers used the wide house-type straw broom until about 1950, when manufacturers developed corn brooms specifically for curling. They were exciting, allowing maximum sweeping effort with a snap and a thump that became a near-deafening chorus when executed by masters. The broom was king at the time and the brush was almost nowhere to be seen in Canada or the United States.

There were some notable Canadian exceptions to the straw broom rule. John Mayer of Calgary copied the Scots in 1965 and began making and using his own version of the brush as lead for the Bruce Stewart team. This team was successful on the cashspiel circuit, and his mixed team of 1971 was the first to use brushes at a Canadian championship.

Curling's all-time bad boy, long-haired Paul Gowsell of Calgary had his team using brushes in 1975 on the way to the World Junior title and domination of the cashspiel circuit.

The Ed Lukowich team broke new ground winning the 1978 Brier. They were the first team to use brushes at a Canadian men's championship.

Canadian curlers laughed at the brush in 1970 and ten years later were lining up to try one. Today Canadian curlers favor the brush over the broom by 9 to 1.

Don Alexander, one of the few curlers in Canada still using the corn broom, gives his broom a drink.

Ice

S cotland's winters were so mild that the first indoor club didn't open until 1907 at Crossmyloof, Glasgow. By contrast, Canadian curlers were literally driven indoors by winter's sub-zero temperatures. Covered rinks popped up in Montreal (1847), Toronto (1859), Hamilton (1860), Ottawa (1868) and Winnipeg (1876).

The first artificial rink built in 1827 by John Cairnie on his grounds at Curling Hall, Largs. Oil painting by McLennen.

Putting in the rings and painting them is painstaking work.

Today artificial ice is made with a refrigeration system coupled with a compressor pumping freon through underground pipes. To an early Scottish curler, artificial ice meant flooding stones or a tarmac to make your own ice, rather than waiting for a pond to freeze over.

Scotsman John Cairnie, first president of the Royal Caledonian Curling Club, pioneered homemade ice in 1827. He built a bed of clay and whinstone chips, which he flooded with a quarter-inch of water, on his grounds at Largs, Scotland. Cairnie noticed that shallow ponds froze faster than deep ones, and found that the rink froze overnight. He later discovered that ice formed almost instantly when water was sprinkled from a watering can, resulting in the first artificial ice and pebble.

Man-made ice improved steadily with technology and curlers were no longer dependent on Jack Frost for their playgrounds. Pond curling became a fad and man-made ice became the norm.

In the old days, as the light of day faded into dusk, candles, lanterns, and torches were lit and skips dangled white handkerchiefs from their brooms to make the target easier to see. Later, car headlights were positioned to light up the loch, until electric lighting gave curlers the luxury of extended play.

Quality indoor ice is considered the strongest single influence in the advancement of curling techniques.

An early type of hack was a strip of sheet-iron secured to the ice. Watercolor by R. M. Alexander.

The Hack

The earliest hack, as the name implies, was a slippery foothold three or four inches deep, hacked into the ice, to make it easier to heave a boulder or a kuting stone.

Later curlers devised a sheet-iron boot attachment with spikes, called a crampit, cramp, or tramp. The drawback of crampits was that when players walked all over the ice with them, they ruined the rink. Eventually the crampit became known as a strip of sheet-iron secured to the ice, allowing curlers a firm push-off.

Different shapes of iron plates were invented including crosses, triangles and horseshoes; one to hold the toe of the front foot and the other, the heel of the trailing foot. These forerunners of the modern rubber hack were known as crisps, triggers, trickers and grippers.

Early hacks were made of wood or steel and by the late 1800s, Canadian curlers started to use rubber.

The present-day hack in Scotland can be either a raised, rubber-covered plate bored into the ice, or a sunken rubber-lined hack, which is used in Canada and in some indoor Scottish clubs. Surprisingly, the Canadian hack has remained virtually unchanged over the last 50 years.

The latest innovation to the hack comes from Montreal curler Marco Ferraro, who consulted with rubber experts, a mathematician and top curlers. Ferraro reasoned that since standard hacks are straight-backed, when the skip targets for a wide shot, curlers wind up with their pushing foot on an angle in the hack and not in a stable position. Ferraro designed his "Marco Hack" with a slight curvature that allows a curler to place his or her foot flat against the back of the hack when lining up with the target, the skip's broom.

Some curlers, like 1989 World champion Pat Ryan of Alberta, complained that the back of the hack was too high and Ferraro later changed the design slightly.

There are an estimated 22,000 hacks in use in the world.

Trickers, forerunners of the modern hack.

The Royal Caledonian "The Mother Club of Curling"

Engraving of John Cairnie.

As curling became more popular in Scotland in the early 1800s, clubs began to be organized, making it necessary to form a governing body.

John Cairnie, who built a curling hall at Largs, Scotland in 1813, was the driving force behind the Royal Caledonian Curling Club, founded in 1838.

With the development of clubs, uniform rules were necessary. The Duddingston Club led the way, in 1804, with "Rules in Curling". These rules were amazingly similar to those followed today and were remarkable for their common sense.

Rules in Curling

I The usual length of a rink is from thirty-six to forty-four yards inclusive; but this will be regulated by circumstances and the agreement of parties. When a game is begun the rink is not to be changed or altered, unless by the consent of the majority of players; nor is it to be shortened, unless it clearly appears that the majority are unable to make up.

II The hog score to be one-sixth part of the length of the rink distant from the tee, and every stone to be deemed a hog the sole of which does not clear the score.

III Each player to foot in such a manner that, in delivering his stone, he brings it over the tee.

IV The order of playing adopted at the beginning must be observed during the whole course of a game.

V All curling-stones to be of a circular shape. No stone is to be changed throughout a game, unless it happens to be broken; and the largest fragment of such stone to count, without any necessity of playing with it more. If a stone rolls or is upset, it must be placed upon its sole where it stops. Should a handle quit a stone in the delivery, the player must keep hold of it, otherwise he will not be entitled to replay the shot.

VI A player may sweep his own stone the whole length of the rink; his party not to sweep until it has passed the hog score at the farther end, and his adversaries not to sweep until it has passed the tee. The sweeping to be always to a side.

VII None of the players, upon any occasion, to cross or go upon the middle of the rink.

VIII If in sweeping or otherwise a running stone is marred by any of the party to which it belongs, it must be put off the ice; if by any of the adverse party, it must be placed agreeable to the direction which was given to the player; and if it is marred by any other means, the player may take his shot again. Should a stone at rest be accidentally displaced, it must be put as nearly as possible to its former situation.

IX Every player to be ready when his turn comes, and to take no more than a reasonable time to play his shot. Should he, by mistake, play with a wrong stone, it must be replaced where it stops by the one with which he ought to have played.

X A doubtful shot is to be measured by some neutral person whose determination shall be final.

XI Before beginning to play, each party must name one of their number for directing their game. The players of his party may give their advice to the one so named, but they cannot control his direction, nor are they to address themselves to the person who is about to play. Each director, when it is his turn to play, to name one of his party to take the charge for him. Every player to follow the direction given to him.

XII Should any question arise the determination of which may not be provided for by the words and spirit of the rules now established, each party to choose one of their number in order to determine it. If the two so chosen differ in opinion, they are to name an umpire, whose decision shall be final.

When the Grand Caledonian Curling Club (renamed the Royal Caledonian Curling Club in 1843), was formed in Edinburgh, Scotland its objective was "to unite curlers throughout the world into one brotherhood of the rink."

The founding of the Royal Club gave curling its first central association and is generally considered the most prominent and far-reaching event in the history of the sport.

Cairnie, an innovator and accomplished curler, bacame the first president of the Grand Caledonian. In 1833, he called on all Scottish clubs to submit lists of their officers, number of curlers and matches played. This became *The Annuals*, an impressive record, compiled regularly since 1839.

The initial membership of the Royal Caledonian was 28 clubs, a number which rose to 655 clubs, or 20,000 curlers by the end of the century.

When the "mother club of curling" became the Royal Caledonian, Prince Albert was named patron. Since then, patrons have been Royal Family members, and since 1900, always a king or queen.

Just as there was a will to develop good sportsmanship, with early curling rules against betting or swearing on the ice, (backed up by a two-shilling fine), the early rules of club meetings reflected some concerns of the day and included:

– that whiskey punch be the usual drink of the club to encourage barley crops.

– that members not talk about politics of church or state.

– that anyone convicted of theft or robbery have his name struck from the membership roll.

– that any member showing up drunk for a meeting leave immediately for the day.

Today the Royal Club has branches and affiliated associations in over twenty countries.

The Canadian Branch of the Royal Caledonian was one of the earliest affiliates of the mother club.

The Grand
Match

The Grand Matches of Scotland began in the frosty winter of 1846-47 when a long cold spell kept the lochs frozen over for nearly three months. Members of the Royal Club had been trying for years to set up a national bonspiel pitting curlers from northern Scotland against curlers from the south.

The first Grand Match. Penicuik, January 15, 1847. Watercolor by Jemimah Wedderburn.

For the event to be held, very thick or "black" ice was required. Curlers were able to play on two inches of pond ice if they didn't stand too close to each other, but to play a Grand Match with hundreds of participants, they needed at least six inches of ice.

On January 15, 1847, curlers traveled by horse, by carriage, by rail and by foot to play the first Grand Match on a loch at Penicuik House, owned by Sir George Clerk. They brought their own stones and brooms with them. The final count was 300 curlers; 68 teams from the south and 12 teams from the north. Surplus curlers from the south arranged a side match amongst themselves. In the main event, with 24 rinks competing, the south edged out the north 238 to 216.

Curlers met, weather permitting, on a shallow man-made loch at Carsebreck, near Stirling for most of the Grand Matches held between 1853 and 1935.

By 1935, the pond at Carsebreck had to be abandoned as a site as it had become too expensive to maintain. The last Grand Match played there attracted more than 2,500 curlers.

The Grand Match has suffered in the mild winters since World War II, with the weather frosty enough for only three of the open air tournaments between 1945 and 1979.

The last Grand Match was played on February 7, 1979 at Lake of Menteith, with 600 teams, or 2,400 curlers taking part. The north beat the south 3937 to 3144.

The last Grand Match.
Lake of Menteith,
February 7, 1979.

Curling
in Canada

Curling Match at Montreal by James Duncan. From "The Illustrated London News", February 17, 1855. National Archives of Canada/C-6738.

Scottish immigrants introduced curling to Canada where it thrived and attained a level of excellence that remains unsurpassed.

The sport evolved significantly from its humble beginnings, in the winter of 1760, when Scottish troops melted down cannon balls to fashion curling irons. Long, harsh Canadian winters were ideal for the game.

By 1807, the first North American club was established. On January 22 of that year, twenty sporting Montreal merchants, who had been curling on the ice of the St. Lawrence River behind Molson's Brewery, founded the Montreal Curling Club. (In 1924, the club was honored with the privilege of adding "Royal" to its name.)

Early rules of the Montreal Club stated that the losing party pay for a bowl of whisky toddy, to be placed in the middle of the table for the rest of the curlers.

A second club was organized at Quebec City in 1821, also using irons. Curlers from each city met halfway on the St. Lawrence River at Trois Rivières in 1836. Quebec won, 31-23, with the losers paying for dinner.

The Montreal and Quebec curling clubs sought affiliation with the Royal Caledonian Curling Club as soon as news of the founding of the Royal Club reached them. They were accepted and named the Canadian Branch of the Royal Caledonian Curling Club in 1852, with headquarters in Montreal. The Canadian Branch still exists as the governing body for curling in eastern Quebec and the Ottawa Valley in eastern Ontario.

Opening of the Thistle Curling Club rink, Montreal. From "Canadian Illustrated News", Vol. III, January 14, 1871. National Archives of Canada/C-54213.

The Ross-Hodgson Annual Curling Match, Saturday, March 4, 1916 at " Woodlands", Lac Brulé, Quebec.

*Stained glass window commemorating the
150th Anniversary of the Royal Montreal Curling Club.*

Curling on the Don River, Toronto, 1860. Public Archives of Canada/C-11234.

Nearly 40,000 people, most of them Scots, settled Ontario between 1816 and 1823. Some of them were stone masons and made their curling stones from granite. Ontario's first curling club was in Kingston (1820). Within five years, the game's popularity had spread to Toronto. Curling clubs sprouted all over the province and the founding of the Toronto Curling Club in 1837 foreshadowed that city becoming the center of curling in Ontario.

Competition between Quebec and Ontario curlers grew and in 1859, with the coming of the Grand Trunk Railway, curlers no longer had to travel days by horse and wagon to compete against each other. The only problem was that Quebec curlers insisted on competing with their irons (used widely in Montreal until 1954), while Ontario curlers wanted to use granite rocks. They compromised by playing separate matches using irons against irons and rocks against rocks. Quebec invariably won the games using irons and Ontario won the games played with rocks.

Curling spread fairly quickly throughout Ontario in the early part of the 19th century. But even though Ontario curling clubs had three times the membership of Quebec clubs, they remained without a policy-making voice until 1874, when they united and joined the Royal Club as the branch of the Province of Ontario.

Curling in High Park, Toronto, 1860.
Public Archives of Canada/C-11233.

Curling on the lakes near Halifax, 1870. Sketch by H.B. Laurence. National Archives of Canada/C-41092.

Curling spread more slowly in the Maritimes. Coal miners from Scotland, with curling stones in tow, settled in Nova Scotia and started clubs in Halifax (1824) and Pictou (1829). Another group of Scots brought the game to Newfoundland, forming a club in St. John's in 1843. New Brunswick sportsmen were inspired to take up curling after reading about the 1853 Grand Match at Carsebreck, Scotland. They imported stones, liked the game and formed a club in 1854. Islanders caught onto the game later and founded a club at Charlottetown, Prince Edward Island in 1887.

Manitoba's first settlers, in 1812, made curling stones from oak blocks. Curling exploded in the west, turning Winnipeg into the center of curling, with more clubs in Manitoba than in Quebec and Ontario combined. The Manitoba Branch of the Royal Caledonian was established in 1888 and curlers from all parts of Canada and the U.S.A. flocked to the Winnipeg Curling Club, with 62 rinks participating in the bonspiel that year.

Small clubs began to pop up all over Saskatchewan after about 1880. They catered to farmers and featured thatched wooden huts to protect curlers and the natural ice from the snow and wind. Before long, Saskatchewan had more curlers than any other province. Early clubs in Saskatchewan, Alberta and British Columbia chose to turn to the Manitoba Branch for guidance.

*Calgary
Ladies Curling
Club, 1919-20.*

The Manitoba Curling Association celebrated its centennial in January 1988. The festivities included a re-enactment of curling as it was 100 years ago.

Championship game: J.T. Lithgow vs Colonel Rourke,
Dawson Curling Club, Yukon, April 1901. (Photo by
Goetzman). National Archives of Canada/PA-52869.

Cold winters drove curling indoors and the bigger clubs began to build indoor rinks after 1840. By 1900, Canadian curling clubs had moved almost exclusively indoors. Indoor rinks, and later, modern ice-making technology brought the sport closer to an art form, eliminating snow, ice bumps and much of the luck that had previously made up the game.

Canada felt the need for its own governing body to regulate the sport and the Dominion Curling Association (later renamed the Canadian Curling Association) was founded in 1935. The C.C.A. was instrumental in promoting the Canadian men's championship and in starting a national high school championship in 1950, a national ladies' championship (1961), mixed (1964), senior men's (1965), junior ladies' (1971) and senior ladies' (1973).

In 1974, the C.C.A. opened a new branch, Curl Canada, to develop a national teaching program. The goal of Curl Canada instructor courses and clinics was to train instructors to teach standardized curling skills and techniques. The initial concept has grown since then to also include coaching certification, ice technicians and club management.

Canada currently has an estimated 1,000,000 curlers and is generally considered the dominating force in both innovations to the sport and competitive curling success.

Poster developed by the Canadian Curling Association to promote 1988 Curl Week.

The Game
Evolves

Then...

Now...

Overseas Tours

In 1858 when the first invitation from Canadian curlers to "come and curl" was sent to Scottish curlers, Scotland was still considered the mecca of curling.

The challenge was finally met in 1902 when six teams of Scottish curlers sailed from Liverpool to play matches in Halifax, St.John, Montreal, Quebec, Ottawa, Toronto, Winnipeg, Minneapolis, St. Paul, Milwaukee, Chicago, Detroit and New York.

The visitors were given the royal treatment; they traveled in luxury dining cars and were wined and dined in the tradition of international goodwill. The North Americans won 252 of 446 games, losing 167 and tying 27.

Canadians made their first tour of Scotland in 1909. A Scottish tour of Canada followed in 1922 and Canadians again traveled abroad in 1949.

Official tours still take place, though they tend to be more for fun, with the real competition reserved for cash bonspiels and world championships.

Teams from Scotland toured North America for the first time in the winter of 1902-03.

SCOTO-CANADIAN CURLING TEAM 1903

The Slide

*The slide delivery - a dynamic
component of the game.*

The slide was one of many revolutionary changes to curling during the 20th century.

For generations curlers had delivered their rocks directly from the hack. The modern slide delivery was born at the St. John's Curling Club in Winnipeg in 1930. The father of the slide was Ken Watson, who won the last of his three Briers in 1949.

Watson said his team discovered the slide one night during a practice session when his lead forgot to slip a rubber onto his shoe before delivering his stone. He skidded crazily with the stone, about twenty feet, and the rest is curling history. The Watson team slid its way to a first Canadian title in 1936. The slide enticed younger curlers to take up what had previously been considered a sport for senior citizens.

Canada had the advantage of set-in hacks, which provided great stability for the push-off slide. By 1945, the slide had changed curling strategy. The draw game was going out of style and the takeout game became the vogue. The slide allowed the curler to stay longer on line with the skip's broom and have greater control over the stone. Watson wrote a recipe for the slide in *Ken Watson on Curling* in 1950 and the book became a bible for generations of curlers to follow.

Since its inception, the slide delivery has confounded rule makers. The Royal Caledonian was concerned about the admissibility of the slide delivery and sounded out member clubs in Canada and the U.S.A. before finally conceding to allow the slide.

Early sliders never slid very far in their deliveries. Even Ken Watson admitted he never released his rock much past the top of the house. The need for a controlling rule, however, became glaringly evident in the 1950s, when Stan Austman of Saskatchewan slid all the way down the sheet of ice and placed his final stone on the button.

Rules which followed included: stopping before the hog line, sliding foot not to touch the hog line and, currently, the stone must be clearly released before the hog line but the slide can continue unlimited after that.

Ken Watson displaying his famous slide.

Mother Country
Versus the Students

Both Scotland (the mother country) and Canada (the student) boasted of having the best teams in the world. The Scotch Whiskey Association finally arranged a Canada-Scotland challenge in 1959, pitting the Scottish champions against the Canadian champions.

The Richardson family from Regina took on Willie Young's team. The first Scotch Cup generated much excitement and controversy. The Richardsons had long slide deliveries, swept with corn brooms from tee line to tee line and played a strong hitting game. Young's Scottish side released their stones before the front circle, swept with brushes only after the hog line and played a draw-style game.

The Canadians won all five games, dumbfounding the Scots with a deadly array of precision takeouts and accurate draws. Stones left short of the house were routinely cleared to make way for the skip's final shot. Lead stones were deliberately thrown through the house as the Canadians protected their score advantage, leading some Scottish fans to cry, "that's nae curling." Like it or not, the course of Scottish curling had been forever changed.

For centuries, Scots had followed the draw game of their forefathers. It was considered unsportsman-like, against the spirit of the game and boorish to strike at opponents' stones. After the initial humiliation at the 1959 Scotch Cup, they chose to fight fire with fire. The Scots developed the slide delivery and the hitting game, and in 1967, Chuck Hay's four-some gave Scotland its first Scotch Cup.

The Richardsons' innovative style of play mesmerized even this young Scottish spectator.

Canada Teaches Europe

With tremendous success in world competition, much of it a result of using new formulas, Canada was considered the trend setter. European countries enviously looked on, striving for the opportunity to compete at the world level, and finally turned to Canadian innovators for help.

Topnotch curlers and instructors such as Ray Turnbull, Wally Ursuliak and Warren Hansen took their curling schools to Europe and taught in countries including Norway, Sweden, France, Germany, Denmark, Finland, Italy and later on parts of the Orient. Eigil Ramsfjell, 1988 Olympic curling gold medalist and co-author of this book, was one of their students.

Warren Hansen directing clinic in Lahr, West Germany, October 1979.

The "students", Duluth, 1976. Left to right, Eigil, Gunnar Sigstadsto, Kristian Soerum, Gunnar Meland.

Strategy Changes

Hec Gervais (left), "the Friendly Giant", (shown here with Harvey Mazinke at the opening ceremonies of the 1987 Edmonton Brier), was a master strategist.

In 1959, when Ernie Richardson beat Willie Young in the first Scotch Cup, Scotland was strictly a draw country, while Canadians were strong in the takeout and draw game. During the next decade, teams such as Ron Northcott's (world champions 1966, 1968, 1969) introduced a crafty draw game coupled with superb takeout ability.

Games were 12 ends, allowing for a more patient strategy (curling was originally 20 ends, then 14, then 12 and now 10). Curlers such as Hec Gervais (Scotch Cup 1961) and Alfie Phillips (Brier 1967) played a new style of draw. They placed guards in front of the rings and then drew around them for protection from subsequent shots. Strategy demanded that skips increase the difficulty of an opposing team's shots because an opponent was no longer expected to miss a wide open takeout in the rings.

Peeling, or clearing front stones became easier with the dominance of the brush in the 1980s. The ice was cleaner with the brushes because corn brooms tended to shed, resulting in a thin layer of mulch that caused rocks to curl more. Straighter ice and

the shorter 10-end game forced teams to stay closer in score with each other since a comeback was more difficult.

Europeans took to the hitting game and soon perfected it. Their keen, straight ice conditions were ideal for this type of game.

Today's curlers must be strong at both hitting and drawing. It's a cat and mouse game, whereby the clever skip tries to set a trap for the other team. All the strategy in the world, however, isn't enough unless the shooting ability is there.

Measuring a stone. Curling is a game of precision.

There is currently a move to make rule changes that would put more rocks into play. Some say that straight ice and strong hitting teams have made curling boring to watch. It is normal for teams with last rock advantage to play takeouts for several consecutive ends, waiting for a miss by their opponents that would allow them to score two points. When this doesn't happen, they hit and roll out of the house or throw their final rock through the house, purposely "blanking" an end in order to retain last rock advantage in the following end. Proposed rule changes, partially followed in the annual Skins game, would force teams who purposely blank ends to lose last rock. It is thought that this change will make teams play more aggressively, to take more chances to try to either score two or more points with last rock or "steal" one or more points without last rock.

While rules for international competition are more or less standard, players looking for different challenges have developed alternate versions of curling, including singles, doubles and points games that award a predetermined number of points for specific shots. The sheet of ice used is criss-crossed with lines and circles, painted on the ice much like a target.

A sheet of ice marked for points' competition.

Straight ice tends to take many of the delicate shots out of the game and it is not uncommon for curlers to ask ice makers to put more "curl" into the ice.

As strategy levels and difficulty of shots increased over the years, so did the length of games. In an effort to speed up games for both players and fans, Ontario's Doug Maxwell introduced a chess-like timeclock at the 1986 Skins game. The clock was first used in international play at the 1989 World Championships in Milwaukee, Wisconsin.

Curlers time a stone as it travels down the ice to determine the amount of force needed for a shot.

The stopwatch is an innovation which predates the timeclock. For years curlers learned the weight, or amount of force needed for a draw shot, by observation and trial and error. The "feel" method remains important, but around 1975, curlers began to time a stone as it traveled down a sheet between designated points. By comparing the time of a rock with times of rocks thrown during previous games, curlers could come up with a precise measurement of how hard they had to throw the stone. If the ice is heavy, or "slow" (not to be confused with the time on the watch), the rock is thrown harder, takes a shorter time to travel the length of the ice and stops quickly. Thus, little time is required. On keen, or "fast" ice, the stone is thrown lightly and makes a slow, deliberate trip down the ice, almost refusing to stop. Thus, more seconds are counted. The stopwatch in now used by most top teams and is a good way to communicate weight between players.

The International Curling Federation

The International Curling Federation evolved out of the need for a modern association that would bring curlers of all countries into "one brotherhood of the rink." The formation of a curling federation was also a prerequisite for the sport to be accepted in the Olympics.

The I.C.F. was formed after a 1966 proposal by Allan Cameron of Scotland. Within a decade, the I.C.F. had become the main curling body at the world level, outgrowing the Royal Club from which it had sprung.

The I.C.F. regroups almost all curling countries and formulates standardized rules for world competition.

Television
Coverage

Canadian television coverage of curling began in 1960 when the Canadian Broadcasting Corporation carried the final draw of the 1960 Brier. In later years, coverage included a late night Brier report and the national and world finals. The annual C.B.C. Classic was instrumental in bringing curling into the living rooms of Canadians by inviting top curlers to compete in televised games.

The Sports Network (T.S.N.) began broadcasting daily draws of the Brier, the Ladies' Scott Tournament of Hearts and some world championships in the 1980s.

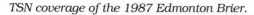
TSN coverage of the 1987 Edmonton Brier.

Bud Somerville, right, winner of the 1974 CBC Curling Classic.

Curling ratings have grown to impressive numbers, with the 1988 Brier final in Chicoutimi, achieving a 38% market share.

CBC CURLING TELEVISION RATINGS 1988

Date	Event	1/4 Hour	%	Reach
March 5	The Scott Tournament of Hearts	551,000	25%	1,318,000
March 12	Labatt Brier (Semi)	619,000	34%	1,148,000
March 13	Labatt Brier (Final)	1,119,000	38%	1,818,000
April 2	Pepsi Juniors	287,000	17%	543,000
April 9	Glayva Ladies' World	278,000	16%	648,000
April 17	World Championship (Semi)	757,000	35%	1,237,000
April 18	World Championship (Final)	814,000	42%	1,447,000

*TSN CURLING TELEVISION RATINGS 1988

Event	Average 1/4 Hour Audience
Skins Game	115,000
The Scott Tournament of Hearts	104,000
Labatt Brier	95,000

* Based on 1.2 million cabled homes.

The Labatt Brier had four champions who went on to win world finals between 1980 and 1986. They were Rick Folk (1980), Al Hackner (1982, 1985), Ed Werenich (1983) and Ed Lukowich (1986). Lukowich approached Jim Thompson of T.S.N. with the idea of setting up a televised playoff between the teams. Thompson suggested a "skins" game, with each end worth a certain amount of money. To win money, teams had to score two points in an end or steal the end without the hammer (last rock advantage). If not, the money would carry over to the next end. Organizers invited subsequent men's and ladies' champions, including Russ Howard (1987), Pat Ryan (1988, 1989), Linda Moore (1985) and Heather Houston (1988) to take part.

The 1987 TSN Skins Game Series in Thunder Bay, Ontario. Left to right, John Ferguson, Tim Belcourt and Glenn Howard compete for big bucks.

Curling
Around the
World

Outdoor curling in Scotland...

and in Canada...

Curling is currently played in some 18 countries (including Canada and Scotland) on four continents.

England, Wales and Ireland

Scotland had more luck getting curling across the Atlantic into Canada than it did transporting it over the English border. There was little curling in England before 1811 when a few Scots curled on a canal north of London. Most curling was between Scots who had moved over the border in the north of England. The first curling club was formed at Leeds in 1820, followed by one founded at Liverpool in 1839. By 1914, there were 37 clubs. The number of curling clubs in England melted away with warm winters. Many players had to travel to Scotland or Switzerland. Today, England counts about 200 curlers and about 14 clubs. There are no permanent curling rinks, but rather hockey rinks used for curling.

Here and on the following page, curling at Buxton, England at the turn of the century.

Wales is a relative newcomer to curling. Welsh curlers opened an ice rink for skating and curling at the Deeside Leisure Centre in North Wales in 1973. The Welsh Curling Association was started in 1974 and joined the Royal Club in 1975. Wales became a member of the European Association in 1978 and sent a men's team to compete in the European Championship in Varese, Italy in 1979. Wales joined the International Curling Federation in 1980 to play in the challenge round of the world championship. There are presently 76 curlers and six clubs in Wales. There is one designated curling rink and two hockey rinks used for curling on specific days.

When curling was introduced to Ireland by Scots in 1839, it met a lukewarm reception, both from sportsmen and from mild winters. James Boomer was coaxed by his friend John Cairnie into making a rink at Belfast. The club was active until Boomer's death in 1846. Irish curling enjoyed a brief revival in the cold winter of 1878-79 but it disappeared by the turn of the century.

United States
Curling Association

U.S.A.

The first organized curling club in the United States was the Orchard Lake Curling Club of Detroit, founded in 1832. Scottish farmers immigrating by boat to Chicago were shipwrecked on the shore of Lake St. Clair. They decided to stay, formed a club and shaped blocks of hickory with which to curl. Soon after, clubs sprang up in New England (Boston 1839), Milwaukee (1843), Chicago (1854) and Wisconsin (where some men improvised by using their wives' irons to curl).

In 1867, twelve clubs got together and calling themselves the Grand National Curling Club, they formed the first American association. By 1880 curling fever had spread westward and 14 clubs joined together to form the North-western Curling Association. The Midwest Association, founded in 1945, represented curlers from Nebraska, Ohio, Wisconsin, Illinois and Michigan.

The first U.S. curling championship was held in 1957 when winners from ten states met on the ice at Chicago Stadium.

The United States Curling Association, amalgamating the United States Men's Curling Association (established in 1958) and the Women's Curling Association (formed in 1947), became the national governing body for the sport in 1976.

U.S. Junior Ladies National Champions, 1989.
Left to right, Erika Brown, Tracy Zeman, Shellie Holerund
and Jill Jones.

There are about 20,000 registered curlers in the U.S., with probably as many once-a-year curlers. The country has 133 clubs playing at 107 rinks and 20 hockey-curling rinks.

The U.S. has had great success in men's world curling competition, boasting four World titles. In 1965, Bud Somerville's rink became the first non-Canadian team to win a world championship. Somerville won again in 1974. Bruce Roberts was successful in 1976 and Bob Nichols' team captured the title in 1978.

Bud's team receives accolades back home after winning the 1967 Scotch Cup, the first of four world titles for the U.S.

Team U.S.A. Bronze medal winners at the World's, Toronto, 1986. Left to right, Steve Brown, Wally Henry, George Godfrey and Richard Maskel.

Sweden

Sweden, like many other European countries, had
a Scottish introduction to the game.

Are, Sweden's most famous winter resort, was a mecca for curling during the years of outdoor curling. The resort was visited by "Father Frost", who baptized new curlers every year.

William Andrew Macfie, a Scot, settled on the Swedish west coast. Macfie introduced curling to the fishing and harbor town of Uddevalla in 1846. The curling club he founded, the Bohuslanka Curlingklubben, still exists as the oldest European club outside Great Britain.

Curling began at Are, the popular winter resort, in 1913, following a visit to Stockholm by four Scottish curlers, who also inspired the forming of the Crown Prince Curling Club, a club which still exists in Stockholm.

His Majesty the King of Sweden,
Carl Gustaf, opens the
European Championship in Vasteras, 1983.

More clubs formed, and in 1916 they founded the Swedish Curling Association. The Association joined the Swedish Sports Confederation in 1955, becoming eligible for government aid.

Swedes organized a national men's championship almost every year after 1917. They started the Swedish Ladies' Championship in 1962, one for junior boys in 1967, and one for junior girls in 1973. There are also Swedish mixed championships, and ones for "oldboys and oldgirls" (over 45) and veterans (over 55).

Sweden has had several men's, women's, and junior world champions, including Kjell Oscarius (1973), Ragner Kamp (1977), and Elisabeth Hogstrom (1981).

Today, 4,500 registered curlers play at 110 curling clubs from Malmo in the south, to Kiruna, north of the Arctic Circle. There are 35 curling rinks, and 23 hockey-curling rinks.

Axel Kamp, president of the Swedish Curling Association and coach of the European and World champions of 1977. Left to right, Bjorn and Hakan Rudstrom, Ragnar Kamp and Christer Martensson.

*Elisabeth Hogstrom
delivers—five-time European
champion, World champion (1981) and
Olympic runner-up (1988).*

Norway

*Parading teams before a Norway-Sweden
game at Lillehammer in the late sixties.*

The earliest record of curling in Norway dates from 1880, but the game did not really catch on until the 1950s. There is evidence of some earlier activity at Finse, where curling stones can still be seen in the foundation of fence posts on the hotel terrace.

Outdoor curling at Oppdal 1956, one of the very first photos of curling in Norway.

Norway receives runner-up prize at the Air Canada Siver Broom, Winnipeg, 1978. This was the first time the Norwegians reached the playoffs in world competition.

In 1954, a Scottish team visited Oppdal, a mountain resort, inspiring a renewed interest in the game. The Norwegian Curling Association was formed in 1956 with Rolf Christensen, who was educated at Glasgow High School, as its first President. Norwegian curling was strictly an outdoor sport until 1969, when Norway's first indoor rink was built in Asker, just outside Oslo.

Despite a lack of indoor facilities, Norway greatly increased its international curling status in the 1970s. With strong support from its National Sports Association, it built an elite curling program (which included Canadian coaching). The results speak for themselves – three world victories in the last ten years.

The country now has more than 1,400 curlers in about two dozen clubs.

Norwegian curlers were double medal winners at the 1988 Calgary Olympics. The men won gold, the women, bronze. (Curling was a demonstration sport.)

Finland

The Mayor of Hyvinkaa, Osmo Antilla, and Terho Toivonen spearheaded the drive to bring curling to Finland in 1969. They led a group that purchased a second-hand set of stones from Sweden and started playing on one lane of natural ice. More teams joined the next year, including one skipped by Isto Kolehmainen who later became the perennial Hyvinkaa champion. The club grew to two sheets, but remained on natural ice for the first five years. Hockey rinks were later used and the club's ice was covered in 1984. The Finnish Curling Association was admitted to the Royal Club in 1978.

Finns compete in the European Curling Championship and host the annual Finnish Bonspiel which attracts some Swedish teams. Facilities available to Finland's 400 curlers are five rinks with a total of seven sheets of ice.

Ed and Finnish juniors curl at Hyvinkaa Curling Club, February 1989.

Denmark

Danish skip Tommy Stjerne shouts command to sweepers at 1986 World Championship in Toronto.

The first Danish club was the Copenhagen Curling Club, formed in 1964. It quickly grew to 50 members and began hosting an international bonspiel for the Mermaid Cup, named for the famous statue of the "The Little Mermaid" that sits on a stone in the harbor at Copenhagen.

Denmark joined the Royal Club in 1967 and formed the Danish Curling Association in 1970. The founding father of Danish curling, Gunnar Stenholm, was first president of the Danish Association. He brought Denmark into the International Curling Federation in 1971 and into World competition in 1973.

Marianne Jorgensen gave Denmark its first world title in 1982, an amazing accomplishment for a country that has only about 500 curlers. There are 13 clubs, one designated curling rink, and seven hockey-curling rinks.

Switzerland

Switzerland's first curling match was played in 1880 at 6,090 feet at St.Moritz. Johannes Badrutt, owner of the St.Moritz Kulm Hotel, was incited to host the game after receiving a gift of four pairs of stones and a Royal Club rule book the previous year from a Scottish visitor. Although the weather was ideal for curling, there wasn't much further growth. But as more and more Scottish and English travelers flocked to the spectacular Alpine resorts, hotels began to offer curling. The first curling club opened at St. Moritz in 1894 and affiliated itself with the Royal Club. By 1914, many hotels offered curling. In 1942, 16 clubs formed the Swiss Curling Association and its first national competition was held one year later.

An early photograph of the Bear Hotel, a very popular resort with curlers.

Arosa, an exquisite setting for curling.

The last 25 years of Swiss curling have been a period of tremendous expansion. From 1964 on, Swiss enthusiasm for the game led to a country-wide boom in the building of artificial ice rinks, including arenas at Berne, Lausanne, Neuchatel and Zurich. Switzerland has more than 8,000 curlers in about 200 clubs. It leads the list in European titles and has become a force on the world scene with World champions including Otto Danieli (1975), Jurg Tanner (1981) and Erika Mueller (1983).

Umpires at work! Left, Ernst Steuri, a curling legend in Switzerland.

A four-legged spectator takes in the "roaring game" at Graubunden.

A curler's paradise.

West Germany

By invitation, Scottish curlers brought the game to Oberhof in 1931 in an attempt to expand the number of winter sports at the world championship games. The first curling club, the International Curling Club of Oberstdorf, was founded in 1959.

Roman Roussell, a German who picked up curling in Switzerland, organized the first competition in Garmisch in 1961. By 1966, 30 German clubs banded together to form the German Curling Association.

Germany first competed in the Scotch Cup in 1967. There were 250 curlers in Germany by 1968 and the figure had doubled to 500 by the time they hosted the Silver Broom at Garmisch in 1972. Keith Wendorf, a Canadian working in Lahr, changed the course of German curling by making Germany a world contender. Wendorf, playing skip, reached the World semi-final twice, and lost the final in 1983. Another transplanted Canadian, Roger Schmidt, skipped Germany to the 1987 World final in Vancouver only to lose to Canada's Russ Howard. Andrea Schopp brought home Germany's first World title in 1988.

Roger Schmidt's team wins semi-final against Norway, Vancouver 1987.

Austria

Seefeld, in the Tyrol, is an ice sports center. It has 40 alpine curling rinks.

The First World War disrupted Austrian curling after it began in Kitzbuhel in 1912. It wasn't until 1955, when the Kitzbuhel Curling Club was founded, that the sport was revived. The Tyrol ski resort of Kitzbuhel remains the center of Austrian curling. The 1964 Winter Olympic Games at Innsbruck brought more attention to curling. By 1984, there were clubs in Gratz, Innsbruck, Kirchberg, Salzburg and Vienna. The Austrian Curling Association was formed in 1980 with the aim of building an arena just for curling. Swiss and German champions were brought over to help train Austrian curlers.

Austria became a member of the International Curling Federation in 1982 and succeeded in qualifying for the men's world competition the following year, the same year that Austrian women first entered world play in Moose Jaw, Sakatchewan. Austria's Gunther Hammelt was the first to play for different countries at the World's competition, curling for David Lampl's German team in 1967 and filling in as a substitute for his country's team at the 1984 Air Canada Silver Broom in Duluth, Minnesota.

Netherlands

The Amsterdam Curling Club was founded in 1961 by curlers playing on an outdoor skating rink. During the 1970s, clubs sprang up in the Hague, Leiden, Rotterdam and Utrecht. The Netherlands Curling Association was founded in 1974 and it joined the Royal Club family the following year. The high cost of icemaking has kept a lid on curling's popularity in the Netherlands; there are only about 400 players.

Men's and women's teams play in the European championships and also the challenge round at the World Championship. The country hosts the annual Windmill Bonspiel.

France

French curling began around 1910 at resorts in the Haute Savoie region in the French Alps. Curling received a boost after it was featured in the 1924 Winter Olympic Games at Chamonix.

Curling activity grew to 50 clubs and the French Federation of Ice Sports became curling's governing body in 1941.

Curlers in Megeve had an artificial ice rink constructed in 1955 and in 1959 the Sporting Club of Megeve was the first French club affiliated with the Royal Club. Curling soon spread to other districts in the French Alps.

Curling at the Olympic Games, Chamonix 1924.

Skip Jean Albert Sulpice captivated crowds with his happy gestures at the 1966 Scotch Cup in Vancouver. It was France's debut at the international level. Pierre Boan, with nine appearances at the World Championships, is considered France's ambassador of curling.

Pebbled ice was introduced to France in 1968. There are presently 300 curlers in France in 15 clubs, playing at four curling rinks and 14 hockey-curling rinks.

Pierre Boan,
France's curler
extraordinaire.

Megeve, at 4,000 feet, has hosted the European, World and World Junior Championships. Haute Savoie remains the center of French curling and open-air curling in the mountains has become a French tradition.

World Championship action, Megeve 1971.

The winning team of the "Coupe de France", May 1989.

Italy

Curling at Cortina, 1920.
Notice the ice skates!

Cortina, the picturesque resort nestled 5,000 feet up in the Dolomites, was the birthplace of Italian curling. Play was halted in 1914, however, with the onset of the war. It was revived in 1953 by hotel owner and curling buff, Leo Menardi who helped start the first two curling clubs in Cortina – the Cristallo Curling Club and the Miramonti Curling Club.

The Italian Curling Association was established in 1971, joining the Royal Club in 1972. An Italian team competed in the World Championship for the first time in 1973. Andrea Pavani has represented Italy a dozen times since then. Italy hosted the European championship in Varese in 1979. A popular bonspiel is the "International Summer Tournament" which has been held annually since 1963. Italy has 400 curlers and 21 clubs, playing at 4 hockey-curling rinks.

Italian team at the 1978 World's,
Winnipeg.

Japan

It is recorded that curling in Japan was first played at Lake Sawa in Nagano Prefecture in 1918. However, it wasn't until 1972 that the first organized competition took place at Lake Tateshina in Nagano. Canada can be credited with helping Japanese curling take root.

A competition was held in Ikeda in 1979 with the help of the Canadian Embassy in Japan and Ikeda's sister city of Penticton, British Columbia. Hokkaido

The Japanese are very keen curlers.

later asked the province of Alberta to send an instructor to help train. Alberta responded by sending Wally Ursuliak of Edmonton, who later became known as the father of Japanese curling. Ursuliak's clinics were a success and did much to speed up the development of the sport. Japan subsequently invited other Canadian champions, including Paul Gowsell and Neil Houston of Calgary, Russ Howard of Penetanguishene, Ontario and Marilyn Darte of St. Catharines, Ontario.

The Tokyo Curling Club opened in 1980 and the Japan Open Bonspiel began in 1982. The Japan Curling Association, formed in 1984, regrouped Ikeda, Takikawa and Tokoro. Hokkaido, Tokyo and Aichi joined the International Curling Federation the same year. There are already 3,000 Japanese curlers playing for 36 clubs at 26 rinks (one indoor, 25 outdoor). There are currently 20 hockey-curling rinks in use. Japanese teams have tried and failed since 1984 to get into the World Championships through the challenge round, but they are improving every year.

*The 5th annual
Japan Open Bonspiel, 1986.*

The Scottish spirit of curling – Japanese style!

Japanese Ladies Curling Championship team, 1989.

Winning team, skipped by Sigenori Sato, at the 6th annual Japan Curling Championship held at Sapporo Makomanai Ice Arena, March 1989.

New Zealand

*Visiting members of the
Royal Club experience
New Zealand curling.*

Scottish immigrants brought their curling stones to New Zealand and founded the first curling club at Dunedin in 1873. Dunedin being too low, offered only about one week of ice a year. A second club was formed at Mount Ida (alt. 2,000 feet) where curlers could enjoy about six weeks of play. By 1886, the number of clubs had grown to seven and the Royal Caledonian added another branch to its roster.

With no indoor facilities, all curling in New Zealand is practiced on natural ice. Geography has limited New Zealand's contact with other curling countries. Their style of play, therefore, reflects the more traditional characteristics of the game. In recent years, a number of curling tours exchanged between Scotland and New Zealand have proved a pleasant experience for both countries.

Australia

There are foggy memories of some curling in Australia in the 1930s. In 1984, Alan Woods' efforts led to the formation of the Australian Curling Association which resolved to make curling more widely accepted and to ready Australians for eventual competition at the world championships and the Olympics.

In 1988, the city of Melbourne held the International Bicentennial Bonspiel which included a contingent of 30 curlers from New Zealand and two from Sweden. Australians hosted the Linda Moore team (gold medalists at the 1988 Calgary Winter Olympics) in July 1989 for a promotional tour. The only Australian curling club at Melbourne has 45 members.

Other Curling Countries

Belgium and Luxembourg are two other members of the International Curling Federation.

Curling has also surfaced, off and on, in such unlikely places as Mexico, Spain, West Africa, South Africa, the U.S.S.R. and China.

Curling at
the Olympics

T he glory of Olympic gold is the incentive that has sparked curling countries to push through much of this century, so far unsuccessfully, for curling to be included as a medal sport in the Olympics.

Curling was introduced as a demonstration sport at the first Winter Olympics in Chamonix, France. Great Britain, Sweden and France took part. It was a walkover for Great Britain, represented by Scots who won their games against Sweden and France 38-7, and 46-4, respectively.

Curling was mysteriously absent from the 1928 Olympics, but the sport reappeared in 1932 at Lake Placid, again as a demonstration sport. The Great Depression weighed too heavily on the European teams and they pulled out. Only Canada and the U.S.A. took part in a hastily arranged eight-team

Curling participants at the first Winter Olympic Games, 1924.

competition. Teams from Manitoba, Northern Ontario, Ontario and Quebec played a four-game round-robin against teams from Connecticut, Michigan, New York and Massachusetts. Canada won 12 of the 16 games, and that was the extent of Olympic curling for more than 50 years to follow.

The VIIIth Olympiad diploma and gold medal won by Willie Jackson, who was on the team representing Great Britain.

1988 – Winter Olympic Games – Calgary, Canada
Curling – A Demonstration Sport

LADIES' TEAMS

Canada

Skip –	Linda Moore
	Lindsay Sparkes
	Debbie Jones
	Penny Ryan
**	Patti Vande

Denmark

Skip –	Helena Blach
	Lone Kristoffersen
	Lene Nielsen
	Malene Krause
**	Lone Bagge

France

Skip –	Annick Mercier
	Agnes Mercier
	Catherine Lefbure
	Andrea Dupont Roc

Germany

Skip –	Andrea Schopp
	Almut Hege-Scholl
	Monika Wagner
	Lore Schopp
**	Suzanne Fink

Norway

Skip –	Trine Trulsen
	Dordi Norby
	Hanne Pettersen
	Mette Halvorsen

Sweden

Skip –	Elisabeth Hogstrom
	Monika Jansson
	Brigitta Sweik
	Marie Henriksson
**	Anette Norberg

Switzerland

Skip –	Cristina Lestander-Wirz
	Barbara Meier
	Christina Gartenmann
	Katrin Peterhans

United States

Skip –	Lisa Schoenberg
	Carla Casper
	Laura Montford
	Erika Brown
**	Diane Brown

**   Denotes the fifth player

MEN'S TEAMS

Canada

Skip –	Ed Lukowich
	John Ferguson
	Neil Houston
	Brent Syme
**	Wayne Hart

Denmark

Skip –	Gert Larsen
	Oluf Olsen
	Jan Hansen
	Michael Harry
**	Steen Hansen

Germany

Skip –	Andreas Kapp
	Florian Zoergibel
	Huber Christoph
	Michael Schaffer
**	Dieter Kold

Great Britain

Skip –	David Smith
	Hammy McMillan
	Mike Hay
	Peter Smith

Norway

Skip –	Eigil Ramsfjell
	Sjur Loen
	Morten Sogaard
	Bo Bakke
**	Tormod Andreassen

Sweden

Skip –	Dan Ola Eriksson
	Anders Thidholm
	Jonas Sjolander
	Christer Nylund
**	Soren Grahn

Switzerland

Skip –	Hanjurg Lips
	Enrico Simen
	Stefan Luder
	Peter Lips

United States

Skip –	Bud Somerville
	Bob Nichols
	Tom Locken
	Bob Christman
**	Bill Strum

A 1986 request by the International Curling Federation resulted in curling receiving the nod as a non-medal sport in the 1988 Calgary Olympics.

The top eight countries in the men's and women's World Championships were invited to the Olympics.

Left to right, John Ferguson (Canada), Sjur Loen and Morten Sogaard (Norway) in round-robin play. The game was a "Battle of the Button".

Norway's Eigil Ramsfjell, spurred on by the saying that "winning silver is like kissing your sister," won gold, though not official gold medals. Hanjurg Lips' Swiss team took home silver, and Canada's Ed Lukowich disappointed home-town fans by settling for bronze. Bud Somerville of the U.S.A. finished fourth.

Norwegian team and fans celebrating
Norway's gold medal performance.
Left to right, Morten Sogaard, Bo Bakke,
Sjur Loen and Eigil.

Canada - Bronze medal winners.
Front, Ed Lukowich, Wayne Hart
Back, John Ferguson, Brent Syme and Neil Houston.

On the women's side, the Canadian foursome skipped by Linda Moore won gold, Elisabeth Hogstrom of Sweden, silver, and Trine Trulsen's team from Norway, bronze.

Curling is penciled in again as a demonstration sport at Albertville, France in 1992, but its Olympic future after that is uncertain. Curling is currently practiced on four continents, but it falls seven countries short of the Olympic rule that states it must be played in 25 countries.

Even if curling can come up with the magic 25 nations, it still has a bundle of red tape to wade through before being recognized alongside hockey, skiing, and bobsledding as a medal sport. The earliest curling could advance to medal ranking is 1998, because Olympic rules state that there can be no new medal sport added unless six years' notice is given to a host site.

"The Sisterhood of Curling" left to right, Trine Trulsen, Lindsay Sparkes, Mette Halvorsen, Debbie Jones and Hanne Pettersen.

Canada's jubilant gold medal winners. Left to right, Linda Moore, Lindsay Sparkes, Debbie Jones, Penny Ryan and Patti Vande.

The World Championships

Lausanne - 1988
(by Eigil Ramsfjell)

*The Malley Ice Stadium
before the first game.*

After our gold medal performance at the Calgary Olympic Games, we realized we had a once-in-a-lifetime opportunity to make it into the curling history books. All we had to do was win again.

I must admit we did not impress anybody with our play in our first three wins against Denmark, Germany and newcomer Finland, skipped by a fellow with curling's longest name, Jussi Uusipaavainiemi.

Our fourth game against Sweden's Soren Grahn was a messy one in many ways; both teams seemed to decide it in different ends, but it came down to last stone in the extra end. I attempted a hit-and-stay. Sjur ordered sweeping almost before I released the stone. Bo applied all his weight immediately, which was too much for his "eight-ender" brush. There was a dry, cracking sound and the next thing I knew Bo was all over the place! Miraculously, Morten managed to keep all parts of Bo and his brush away from the stone and we won the game.

In our next four games, I played my all-time worst. First against Scotland, who had managed to shake off their "007" image (0 wins, 0 draws, 7 defeats) from the Olympics and were virtually assured a play-off spot, and then against Canada's Pat Ryan, who was extending his defeatless record with each game. My performance did not improve until we played Switzerland, who along with us, was still in the running, as was Canada and Scotland.

Our semi-final against Scotland was to be played first, to accommodate television transmission to Canada of their semi-final against Switzerland in the evening. My percentage score improved 300% against Scotland. I only missed a peel in the 8th end, but by that time the game was pretty much over – we had the hammer and were four up. In my tenth World Championship appearance, we had qualified for my fifth final, after my eigth semi-final.

Norway scores 32% against Canada in the round-robin match. Left to right, Sjur Loen, Morten Sogaard, Bo Bakke and Eigil.

Meanwhile, Pat Ryan was extending his winning streak to 26. When we showed up in the Malley Ice Stadium, Canada needed to steal in the 10th. Swiss skip Daniel Model had to draw to the four-foot to win, but was light and the familiar sound of silencing cowbells was thundering. Our "medicine man", Bo, extremely superstitious when it comes to curling, hurried down to the ice where color of stones for the final was to be decided. We have always won in red and since Canada played white in their semi-final, Bo's wish came true.

At breakfast the next morning, Sjur was sneezing and the butterflies in Bo's stomach had given way to eagles. All was "normal" before the final. After a short stroll along scenic Lake Leman, with the fashionable city of Lausanne on one side and the snow-covered Alps rising on the other, we were ready for action.

Arriving at the stadium for the final.

IOC president, Juan Antonio Samaranch, threw the opening rock. Canada was awarded last-stone-advantage as a result of their round-robin record. Their strategy was cautious, leaving it up to us to take the chances. We scored two by freezing game in the 2nd but they replied immediately. The score was 3-2 after four ends.

We tried every offensive trick we knew; playing corner guards early and freezes later in the ends. Both teams were playing brilliantly. Our freezes were close to perfect and so were Canada's peels. The only slip came in the 6th end when Randy Ferbey half-hit our shot onto their second behind cover. Sjur's come-around was perfect. We were lying two behind cover. Pat attempted a freeze/tap-back with his first, but wrecked. My first was a draw to the top of the four-foot, also behind cover. All Pat had left was one stone and he was looking at three perfectly guarded red shots. His options were either a soft double-takeout attempt, giving us at least two, or a heavy raise-takeout. He chose the latter and played the most brilliant shot I have ever witnessed. Without sweeping, his rock hit the guard and, suddenly, all red shots started moving, none of them stopped in the circles. There was only one stone left, yellow, on the four-foot and half-covered. Canadian second, Don Walchuk set a world record in triple high jumps on ice!

Pat Ryan in command.

105

Eigil's reaction to Pat's brilliant shot in the sixth.

I lifted my chin from my chest and went to congratulate Pat — he neither replied nor changed his sphinx-like expression. The fans, however, were ecstatic and their "Go Canada Go!" did not subside for minutes.

Our go-ahead came in the 8th end. I had a chance for two if I could only make a double-kill on my last shot. Running down the ice, the out-turn was wide all the way. The swing was big after hog and what looked like a steal for 30 metres turned out to be a longed-for deuce and control of the game.

Fate was against us once more in the 9th. Sjur's last stone picked a hair and hit the divider, setting them up with a deuce. I asked Bo to get in touch with The Great Curler Above — his prayers were heard. Pat's shot hit and rolled out and he had to settle for a single point.

In the final end, the eagles in Bo's stomach got the better of him — he missed both his peel attempts. The tension was mounting. We tried to keep center line open, but failed. Pat made a fine draw with his last stone. I decided to go for the winner on out-turn. It was a great sensation to watch the stone curl to its destination and give Norway its third world championship. In eight weeks we had achieved something that will not be repeated for at least four years and possibly, never again.

1988 — what a year for Norway!

The Scotch Cup
(1959 -1967)

The Richardsons proudly bring home the first Scotch Cup, 1959. The "Curling Machine" from Saskatchewan won the World Championship four times, a record.

Bud Somerville's rink broke Canada's six-year winning streak in 1965.

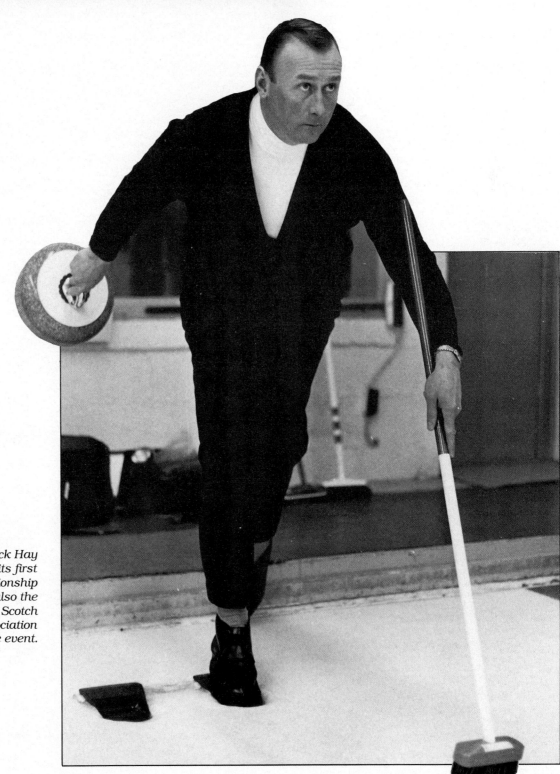

The legendary Chuck Hay skipped Scotland to its first and only World Championship in 1967. It was also the last year that the Scotch Whiskey Association sponsored the event.

Air Canada Silver Broom (1968 -1985)

Ron Northcott, three-time World champion, and the only skip to win both the Scotch Cup (1966) and the Silver Broom (1968, 1969).

Don Duguid won back-to-back World titles in 1970-71, an accomplishment which has not been repeated since then.

1972 - Garmisch, West Germany saw the most controversial World Championship final ever played. Bob Labonte of the U.S. (center) appeared to have won in the 10th end, as Dave Romano (right) of Canada looks on. Labonte's third, Frank Aasand (left) jumps for joy...

Labonte rushed in, lost his balance and kicked the Canadian stone as he fell. Canada tied the game on a measurement and went on to win in an extra end. Labonte felt robbed and swore that Canada would never again win a World championship. The "curse of Labonte" held true for seven years, until Rick Folk won in 1980.

Roland Schneider is ecstatic over Switzerland's first World championship in 1975.

Joe Roberts' unorthodox slide delivery. 1976 Silver Broom, Duluth, Minnesota.

Scotland's Bill Muirhead delivers last stone in the final against the U.S.A...

But, it being the U.S. bicentennial, Bruce Roberts' rink was destined for the victory stand.

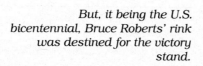

1978: Opening ceremonies, Winnipeg, where the seven-day event drew a record attendance of 102,000.

1980: Tom Wilson, second for Rick Folk's team, and fans celebrate Canada's world win and the breaking of "the curse of Labonte".

1984 — Duluth: Claude Taylor, president of Air Canada, presents the coveted Silver Broom to Eigil's team, a second world title for Norway.
The airline's sponsorship ended in 1985, after eighteen years. The curling world extends their gratitude to Air Canada for their massive contribution to the sport.

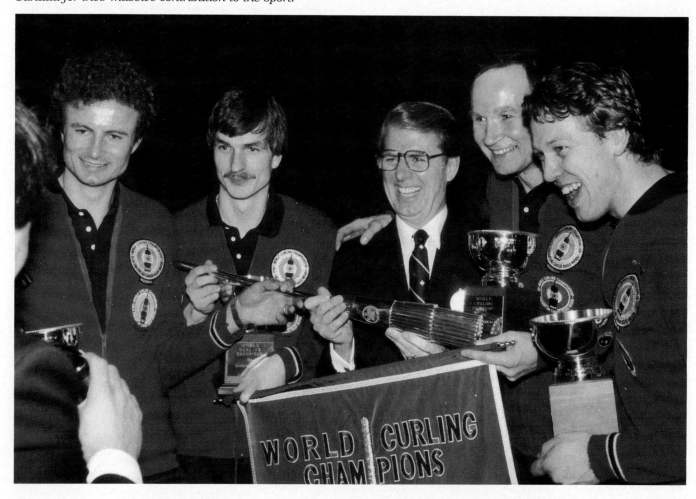

IOC President's Cup
(1986 -1988)

1986 — Toronto: Brent Syme, Neil Houston, John Ferguson and Ed Lukowich with the new World's trophy, the IOC President's Cup, sponsored by Hexagon Curling International.

1987 — Vancouver: Russ Howard's team keeps the Cup at home for another year.
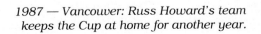

In 1989, the men's and ladies' World Championships were held at the same time, in Milwaukee. Canada was a double winner! Left to right, Heather Houston, Lorraine Lang, Diane Adams, Tracy Kennedy; Pat Ryan, Randy Ferbey, Don Walchuk, Don McKenzie.

Ladies' Curling

The Curlers.

One of the earliest records of a ladies' curling match is
this water color by A.A.A. The Countess of Eglinton
and friends, Eglinton Castle, 1860.

*Organized ladies'
competitions began at the
turn of the century, but the
World Championship was
not established until 1979.
Shown here, the Lachine
Ladies' Curling Club, 1903.*

1985 World champions, Canada's Linda Moore (left) and Debbie Jones.

Spunky Marilyn Darte skipped Canada to the World Championship in 1986.

1988 World champions from Germany. Left to right, Andrea Schopp, Almut Scholl, Suzanne Fink and Monika Wagner.

World Junior Championships

The World Junior Men's championship, sponsored by Uniroyal, began in 1975. Jan Ullsten of Sweden was the first winner. Paul Gowsell of Canada won in 1976 and 1978, and is the only skip to have won more than one World Junior Championship. Canada has won more World junior titles (six) than any other country, and Scotland is next with four. Other winners include the U.S.A. and Sweden.

Canada's Paul Gowsell (right) is the only skip to have won two world Junior Championships (1976, 1978).

Scotland won its fourth World Junior title in 1987. Left to right, Billy Andrew, Douglas Dryburgh, Philip Wilson and Lindsay Clark.

Junior curling, known as young boys' or schoolboys' curling, thrived in the 1950s and '60s. Interest in the sport waned and it was dropped from many high school curriculae, in favor of more conventional sports. The development of smaller, lighter stones has, and should continue to attract younger players to the game, and should, in the long run, improve the calibre of junior curling.

Sweden's (left to right) Peter Lindholm, Johan Hansson, Magnus Swartling and Peter Narup chalked up a third World championship for their country in 1989.

The first World Junior Ladies' Championship was played in Chamonix, France in 1988. Canada's Julie Sutton won in 1988, and Ladawn Funk kept the Canadian winning streak going in 1989.

Teams parade through the streets of Chamonix, France.

Canada won the World Junior title for a second time in 1989. Left to right, Laurelle Funk, Sandy Symyrozum, Cindy Larsen and Ladawn Funk.

The Brier

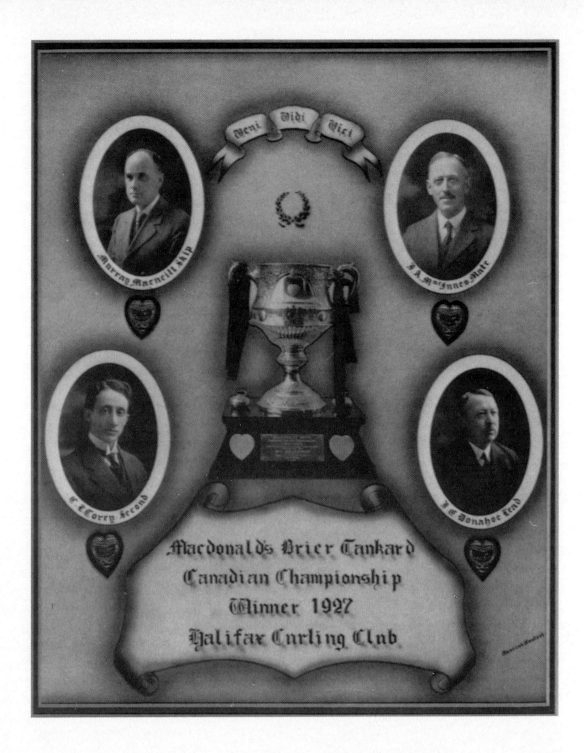

The very mention of the Canadian Curling Championship, the Brier, sends shivers up and down the spine of every curler. The value of winning the right to wear a purple heart crest, emblem of a provincial championship, and a Brier appearance, cannot be measured. Playing in the Brier is an unattainable dream for many and the accomplishment of a lifetime for some.

In 1924, a representative of Macdonald Tobacco traveled from Winnipeg to Montreal to persuade head office to sponsor an east-west curling competition that he was sure would help unite the country. George J. Cameron convinced Macdonald executives to donate a trophy, to be called the Macdonald Brier Tankard.

The first championship was held in 1927. Eight teams were invited to the Toronto Granite Club: Montreal, Toronto, Nova Scotia, New Brunswick, Quebec, Ontario, Northern Ontario and Saskatchewan. Murray Macneill of Halifax, Nova Scotia won the first national title, with a record of six wins and one loss. Teams from Manitoba won a record five consecutive Briers from 1928 to 1932.

City representation was dropped in 1932 in favor of provincial representation and in 1936 Prince Edward Island and British Columbia joined the Brier field.

The first Brier outside of Toronto was in Winnipeg in 1940 and included nine provinces and Northern Ontario. Howard Wood rewarded home town fans with Manitoba's ninth Canadian Championship.

World War II was enough to suspend Brier play, but not enough to keep people away when it returned to Saskatoon in 1946. More than 22,000 fans packed the Saskatoon Arena through the week. Billy Rose fought through tie-breakers against Manitoba and Northern Ontario, giving Alberta the Brier Tankard. Between 1947 and 1971, Garnet Campbell of Saskatchewan was the first dean of the Brier, logging ten appearances. Skip Ken Watson made his last Brier appearance in 1949, going undeafeated at 9-0 to become the first triple Brier winner. Watson had also won the 1936 and 1942 Briers.

A team from Newfoundland, skipped by Thomas Hallett, made its first Brier appearance in 1951, but it wasn't until 1976 that Jack MacDuff gave Newfoundland its first and only Brier victory. Nova Scotia, the host province, won the 1951 Brier with a 10-0 record.

Saskatchewan's contribution to the curling world (left to right) — Garnet Campbell (10 Brier appearances); Harvey Mazinke (1973 Brier champion); Ernie Richardson (4 Briers and 4 World Championships); Rick Folk (broke Canada's seven-year losing streak by winning 1980 World's).

Ron "The Owl" Northcott accepting his third Macdonald Brier trophy, Oshawa 1969.

Superstars that emerged from Briers of the '60s and '70s include Hec Gervais of Edmonton, who, with Ron Anton at third won Briers in 1961 and 1974. Manitoba's Terry Braunstein won the 1965 Saskatoon Brier and his third, Don Duguid, went on to back-to-back Brier glories of his own in 1970 and 1971. Ron Northcott of Alberta was also a star of the '60s, winning Briers in 1966, 1968 and 1969, with different thirds, but constant support from second, Bernie Sparkes and Fred Storey at lead.

When it comes to Brier glory, the accomplishments of the Richardsons, more than a quarter-century ago, stand above all. Regina's Ernie Richardson, with Arnold, Sam, Wes, and Mel Perry in 1963, is the only skip to win four Briers (1959, 1960, 1962, and 1963), an outstanding achievement in sports history.

The pageantry of the Brier — opening ceremonies, Brandon, 1982.

Al Hackner's team made an astounding comeback to win the 1985 Moncton Brier. The sudden-death final against Pat Ryan's team has been rated as one of the most exciting in the history of the Brier.

In 1977, the same year that Jim Ursel gave Quebec its first and only Brier victory, Macdonald Tobacco announced it would withdraw its sponsorship after the 50th Brier in 1979. The Canadian Curling Association struck a deal with Labatt Breweries to take over sponsorship of the 1980 Brier. Winnipeg's Barry Fry won the last Macdonald Brier and Saskatchewan's Rick Folk won the first Labatt Brier in 1980.

One of the innovations introduced by Labatt's is that the round robin competition is followed by a sudden-death semi-final and final, to make the Brier finish more exciting for television. New Brier stars like Pat Ryan and Al Hackner emerged in the 1980s.

In 1981, twenty-two year old Kerry Burtnyk of Manitoba became the youngest player to win a Brier. One of the best clutch shots in Brier history led to a second Canadian championship for Al Hackner in 1985. The "Iceman" made a thin double takeout to tie the final against Pat Ryan of Alberta and went on to win in an extra end. Fate finally paid back Ryan in 1988 when Saskatchewan's Eugene Hritzuk, with a two-point lead going into the last end of the final, folded, giving up three points to an incredulous Ryan. And Ryan didn't even have to throw his last rock!

*Prime Minister
Brian Mulroney
opens 1986 Kitchener-Waterloo Brier.
On the left, Al Hackner, winner 1985 Brier;
on the right, Ed Werenich, winner
1983 Brier.*

Brier attendance peaked at a record 151,538 in 1989, as the curling-crazy city of Saskatoon hosted the 60th Brier, which organizers appropriately called "Magic on Ice". Pat Ryan again triumphed, becoming the first skip since Don Duguid to win consecutive Canadian championships. The modern dean of the Brier is Bernie Sparkes of B.C., who has played in a record 12 Briers, the last one in Edmonton in 1987.

The Brier has seen a number of controversies throughout its 60-year history. There was a flurry of rule-changing in 1928, when Joe Heartwell won the Alberta playdowns. After losing in Saskatchewan, he jumped the border, making it necessary for a rule restricting a team to one playdown per year.

Then there was Ken Watson's slide, first greeted as an unfair advantage, and a later debate over the amateur status of curling. Curlers in the west were competing for larger and larger prizes, even cars, and some argued that the Brier should be limited to amateurs. Organizers defeated a 1964 proposal to limit a Brier curler's winnings to $150.00.

Briers of the 1980s saw more emphasis put on officiating, as judges began to pull rocks from play when curlers committed hog-line violations. Judges also began watching for sweeping and brushing violations. This caused a number of arguments, as players accused officials of getting too involved in the outcome of games in what was traditionally a self-regulating sport.

Earle Morris has the distinction of representing three different provinces at the Brier: Ontario, Quebec and Manitoba.

The tradition of the Brier is unequalled in Canadian sport. Diehard fans travel from city to city, from Brier to Brier to partake in the Brier atmosphere of fellowship, as much as to watch what has been called the premiere event in curling, even outranking the World Championship in spectator attendance and quality of curling.

Bernie Sparkes
— 12 Brier appearances,
the most ever!

The "Bluenoses", fans
from Nova Scotia at the
1987 Edmonton Brier.

Some fans never
miss a Brier...

The 1989 Saskatoon Brier broke all
attendance records; the week-long
"Magic on Ice" attracted 151,538
spectators.

Canadian Ladies' Championships

The forebearer to the Canadian Ladies' Curling Championship was an East-West competition. Prior to 1960, British Columbia, Manitoba, Alberta and Saskatchewan played in the annual Western Canada Championship under the sponsorship of the T. Eaton Company Limited. In 1960, as the Canadian Ladies Curling Association was being formed, an Eastern Canada Championship was held. Ruth Smith of Lacolle, Quebec won the first and only Eastern Canada Championship but lost to Joyce McKee of Saskatoon in the East-West Invitational match.

McKee and her Saskatoon foursome won the first ten-province women's competition and the Dominion Diamond D Trophy in 1961. The women's competition was finally a truly national one.

The women's championship grew and teams from the west continued to dominate. The championship suffered the loss of Dominion Stores' sponsorship in 1967. The Canadian Ladies' Curling Association paid the tab until 1972 when Macdonald Tobacco, the men's major sponsor, expanded its curling involvement to include the Ladies' Championship. The Macdonald Lassie competition enjoyed further growth, accepting an eleventh entry, a team from the Yukon/Northwest Territories in 1976. The C.L.C.A. managed to stage successful championships in 1980 and 1981, despite the loss of Macdonald Tobacco's sponsorship in 1979.

Scott Paper Limited took a chance on the Ladies' Championship in 1982 and continues to sponsor the Scott Tournament of Hearts. The Tournament of Hearts broke new ground in 1985. In an effort to spark fan interest, organizers invited Canadian Ladies' champions to return the year after their win, under the colors of Team Canada. This was to ensure that a Canadian champion would make it back to the following year's championship, necessary because even the best teams seldom repeated provincial championships back-to-back. Heather Houston of Thunder Bay was the first to return skipping Team Canada and win consecutive Canadian Championships.

Connie Laliberte skipped Manitoba to its fourth national championship in 1984.

The Scott Tournament of Hearts marked a new, more exciting era of Canadian women's curling. Canadian champion (1982), turned broadcaster, Colleen Jones of Nova Scotia turned heads when she walked onto the ice at the World Championship wearing a Walkman-style radio and Marilyn Darte of Ontario (1986) made headlines as much for her loud on-ice antics, as her super-short mini-kilt. But the color introduced to women's curling should not overshadow the curling talents of recent Canadian champions, who won five out of six World Curling Championships between 1984 and 1989.

Alberta team with Scott Paper mascot. Left to right, Susan Seitz, Judy Lukowich, Judy Erickson and Betty McCracken.

The team from British Columbia show who's number one in 1987. Left to right, Georgina Hawkes, Pat Sanders, Louise Herlinveaux and Deb Massullo.

Canadian Senior Championships

The Canadian Senior Men's (over 50) Curling Championship began in 1965, with the backing of Joseph E. Seagram and Sons Limited. Senior men representing the provinces competed for the Seagram Stone Trophy from 1965 to 1974. Since Seagram pulled out in 1973, the winners have received medals and prizes from the Canadian Curling Association. Just as the success of junior curlers is often telling of later glory, many of the seniors who have won the national title are familiar to curling fans for their earlier Brier exploits. They include Alfie Phillips of Ontario, Ken Weldon of Quebec, and Art Lobel and Joe Gurowka of Ontario. Skip Lloyd Gunnlaugson of Manitoba is a standout in seniors' play, having won consecutive Canadian Senior Championships in 1982, 1983 and 1984.

The Canadian Senior Ladies' Championship was started in 1973 and continues without a sponsor, as a competition of the Canadian Ladies' Curling Association. The over-50 competition has produced its own cast of stars including four-time winner Flora Martin of British Columbia (1974, '75, '79, '80) and Ev Krahn of Saskatchewan who, with Twyla Widdifield, Shirley Little, and June Kaufman, won three straight Canadian Senior Championships from 1984 to 1986.

1981 Canadian Senior champions from Quebec. Left to right, Jim Wilson, Bert Skitt, Garth Ruiter and George Brown.

Forces in Curling

Curling is called "curling" because of the arc, or curl, that a stone makes as it completes its trip from a curler's hand to the opposite end of the ice. It is amazing that anyone can actually make a rock end up where they want to when you figure that they are shooting it at a twelve-foot target one hundred feet away.

There are many forces weighing upon a traveling rock, including ice conditions, sweeping and how hard the rock is thrown. Because it is not possible to accurately throw a straight rock, a curler always twists the rock's handle clockwise (in-turn), or counter-clockwise (out-turn). A thrown rock will travel relatively straight for the first half of the ice and begin to curl more as it slows.

Forces that produce the curl in curling.

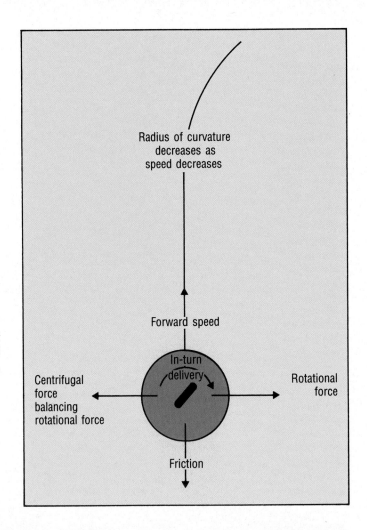

Radius of curvature decreases as speed decreases

Forward speed

In-turn delivery

Centrifugal force balancing rotational force

Rotational force

Friction

Ed Werenich

Al Hackner

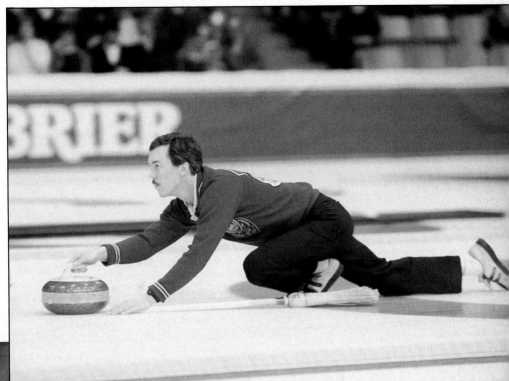

Pat Ryan

Linda Moore

A future champion...?

Eigil Ramsfjell

*Newfoundland's
Blake Fizzard*

Sweeping does not speed up a rock, but it does help it maintain momentum, by wearing down frost on the ice that increases friction and by cleaning the path of the rock. Good sweepers always "dust" the path of a traveling rock to make sure that it picks up no debris. A brush hair or loose straw from a broom can cause a stone to go drastically off course. Sweeping also keeps a rock on a straighter course, by wearing down the ice surface, giving the running edge of the rock less to grab onto as it turns. A made curling shot is the result of the skip holding his broom as a target in the proper place, the deliverer throwing the correct turn and weight and the sweepers judging the traveling weight while the others watch the line. This is why curling is truly a team sport.

Left to right, Bill Strum, Al Gagne and Tom Wright of the U.S.A.

Newfoundland's Eugene Trickett (left) and Rob Thomas

The art of sweeping,
Chamonix, 1924.

*Quebec's Dan Belliveau
(left) and Andrew Carter*

*Left to right, Bill Oliver, Douglas
MacDonald and Wade Blanchard
from New Brunswick*

The Game
Face

Curling harnesses the strategy of chess, the grace of ballet, the cunning of poker and all of the ups and downs of a lovers' quarrel. Curlers' faces reflect some of the oddest expressions seen in sport. Hopes live and die in the seconds between the release of a stone and the time it comes to rest, regardless of the stakes involved. Some, like gamblers in the old west, refuse to let their faces reveal their weaknesses. Others are so caught up that they lose control, their faces contorted and their bodies trembling as they plead with the rock with body language, to follow their commands. Curlers have many game faces and no two are alike.

Anticipation

*Intense
concentation*

The tension and pressure of a big game can fray the nerves and shake up even the best player.

Anxiety

The
(Eight)
End

The eight-ender is one of the most elusive accomplishments in curling. Some say scoring the maximum eight points in one curling end is a tougher feat than the hole-in-one in golf. Not only do you have to make all of your shots to score an eight-ender, but you have to count on the other team to miss most of theirs.

The team of (left to right) Ross Wilson, Wilma Wilson, Shirley Ellison and Ray Field are all smiles after scoring an eight-ender during weekly mixed play at the Lachine Curling Club in Lachine, Quebec. Incredibly, they went on to lose the game 11-10 to clubmate Erwin Rutsch.

Records

World Champions (Men)

Scotch Cup Champions

1959	Canada	Ernie Richardson, Arnold Richardson, Sam Richardson, Wes Richardson
1960	Canada	Ernie Richardson, Arnold Richardson, Sam Richardson, Wes Richardson
1961	Canada	Hector Gervais, Ray Werner, Vic Raymer, Wally Ursuliak
1962	Canada	Ernie Richardson, Arnold Richardson, Sam Richardson, Wes Richardson
1963	Canada	Ernie Richardson, Arnold Richardson, Sam Richardson, Mel Perry
1964	Canada	Lyall Dagg, Leo Hebert, Fred Britton, Barry Nalmark
1965	U.S.A.	Bud Somerville, Bill Strum, Al Gagne, Tom Wright
1966	Canada	Ron Northcott, George Fink, Bernie Sparkes, Fred Storey
1967	Scotland	Chuck Hay, John Bryden, Alan Glen, David Howie

Air Canada Silver Broom Champions

1968	Canada	Ron Northcott, Jimmy Shields, Bernie Sparks, Fred Storey
1969	Canada	Ron Northcott, Dave Gerlach, Bernie Sparkes, Fred Storey
1970	Canada	Don Duguid, Rod Hunter, Jim Pettapiece, Bryan Wood
1971	Canada	Don Duguid, Rod Hunter, Jim Pettapiece, Bryan Wood
1972	Canada	Orest Meleschuck, Dave Romano, John Hanesiak, Pat Hailley
1973	Sweden	Kjell Oscarius, Bengt Oscarius, Tom Schaeffer, Boa Carlman
1974	U.S.A.	Bud Somerville, Bob Nichols, Bill Strum, Tom Locken
1975	Switzerland	Otto Danieli, Roland Schneider, Rolf Gautschi, Ueli Mulli
1976	U.S.A.	Bruce Roberts, Joe Roberts, Gary Kleffman, Jerry Scott
1977	Sweden	Ragner Kamp, Hakan Rudstrom, Bjorn Rudstrom, Christer Martensson
1978	U.S.A.	Bob Nichols, Bill Strum, Tom Locken, Bob Christman
1979	Norway	Kristian Soerum, Morten Soerum, Eigil Ramsfjell, Gunnar Meland
1980	Canada	Rick Folk, Ron Mills, Tom Wilson, Jim Wilson
1981	Switzerland	Jurg Tanner, Jurg Hornisberger, Patrick Loertscher, Franz Tanner
1982	Canada	Al Hackner, Rick Lang, Bob Nicol, Bruce Kennedy
1983	Canada	Ed Werenich, Paul Savage, John Kawaja, Neil Harrison
1984	Norway	Eigil Ramsfjell, Sjur Loen, Gunnar Meland, Bo Bakke
1985	Canada	Al Hackner, Rick Lang, Ian Tetley, Pat Perroud

World Curling Champions

1986	Canada	Ed Lukowich, John Ferguson, Neil Houston, Brent Syme
1987	Canada	Russ Howard, Glenn Howard, Tim Belcourt, Kent Carstairs
1988	Norway	Eigil Ramsfjell, Sjur Loen, Morten Sogaard, Bo Bakke
1989	Canada	Pat Ryan, Randy Ferbey, Don Walchuk, Don McKenzie

World Champions (Ladies)

1979	Switzerland	Gaby Casanova, Rosie Manger, Linda Thommen, Betty Bourguin
1980	Canada	Marj Mitchell, Nancy Kerr, Shirley McKendry, Wendy Leach
1981	Sweden	Elisabeth Hogstrom, Carina Olsson, Birgitta Sewick, Karin Sjogran
1982	Denmark	Marianne Jorgenson, Helena Blach, Astrid Birnbaum, Jette Olsen
1983	Switzerland	Erika Mueller, Barbara Meyer, Barbara Meier, Christina Wirz
1984	Canada	Connie Laliberte, Chris More, Corinne Peters, Janet Arnott
1985	Canada	Linda Moore, Lindsay Sparkes, Debbie Jones, Laurie Carney

World Champions (Ladies) – cont'd

1986	Canada	Marilyn Darte, Kathy McEdwards, Chris Jurgenson, Jan Augustyn
1987	Canada	Pat Sanders, Georgina Hawkes, Louise Herlinveaux, Deb Massullo
1988	Germany	Andrea Schopp, Almut Scholl, Monika Wagner, Suzanne Fink
1989	Canada	Heather Houston, Lorraine Lang, Diane Adams, Tracy Kennedy

World Junior Men's Champions

1975	Sweden	Jan Ullsten, Mats Nyberg, Anders Grahn, Bo Soderstrom
1976	Canada	Paul Gowsell, Neil Houston, Glen Jackson, Kelly Stearne
1977	Canada	Bill Jenkins, John Scales, Sandy Stewart, Alan Mayhew
1978	Canada	Paul Gowsell, John Ferguson, Doug MacFarlane, Kelly Stearne
1979	U.S.A.	Don Barcome, Randy Darling, Bobby Stalker, Earl Barcome
1980	Scotland	Andrew McQuistin, Norman Brown, Hugh Aitken, Dick Adams
1981	Scotland	Peter Wilson, Jim Cannon, Roger McIntyre, John Parker
1982	Sweden	Soren Grahn, Niklas Jarund, Henrik Holmberg, Anders Svennerstedt
1983	Canada	John Base, Bruce Webster, Dave McAnerney, Jim Donahoe
1984	U.S.A.	Al Edwards, Mark Larson, Dewey Basley, Kurt Disher
1985	Canada	Bob Ursel, Brent Mendella, Gerald Chick, Mike Ursel
1986	Scotland	David Aitken, Robin Halliday, Peter Smith, Harry Reilly
1987	Scotland	Douglas Dryburgh, Philip Wilson, Lindsay Clark, Billy Andrew
1988	Canada	Jim Sullivan, Charles Sullivan, Craig Burgess, Dan Alderman
1989	Sweden	Peter Lindholm, Magnus Swartling, Johan Hansson, Peter Narup

World Junior Ladies' Champions

| 1988 | Canada | Julie Sutton, Judy Wood, Susan Auty, Marla Geiger |
| 1989 | Canada | Ladawn Funk, Sandy Symyrozum, Cindy Larsen, Laurelle Funk |

Summary of World Championships Won (Country)

	World Men's	World Ladies'	World Junior Men's	World Junior Ladies'	Total
Canada	19	6	6	2	33
Switzerland	2	2	–	–	4
Sweden	2	1	3	–	6
Denmark	–	1	–	–	1
Norway	3	–	–	–	3
France	–	–	–	–	–
Italy	–	–	–	–	–
Scotland	1	–	4	–	5
Finland	–	–	–	–	–
U.S.A.	4	–	2	–	6
Germany	–	1	–	–	1
England	–	–	–	–	–
Netherlands	–	–	–	–	–
Number of years held	31	11	15	2	–

Canadian Men's Champions

Macdonald Brier Champions

Year	Province	Team
1927	Nova Scotia	Murray Macneill, Al MacInnes, Cliff Torey, Jim Donahoe
1928	Manitoba	Gordon Hudson, Sam Penwarden, Ron Singbusch, Bill Grant
1929	Manitoba	Gordon Hudson, Don Rollo, Ron Singbusch, Bill Grant
1930	Manitoba	Howard Wood, Jimmy Congalton, Victor Wood, Lionel Wood
1931	Manitoba	Bob Gourlay, Ernie Pollard, Arnold Lockerbie, Ray Stewart
1932	Manitoba	Jimmy Congalton, Howard Wood, Bill Noble, Harry Mawhinney
1933	Alberta	Cliff Manahan, Harold Deeton, Harold Wolfe, Bert Ross
1934	Manitoba	Leo Johnson, Lorne Stewart, Linc Johnson, Marno Frederickson
1935	Ontario	Gordon Campbell, Don Campbell, Gord Coates, Duncan Campbell
1936	Manitoba	Ken Watson, Grant Watson, Marvin McIntyre, Charles Kerr
1937	Alberta	Cliff Manahan, Wes Robinson, Ross Manahan, Lloyd McIntyre
1938	Manitoba	Ab Gowanlock, Bung Cartmell, Bill McKnight, Tom Knight
1939	Ontario	Bert Hall, Perry Hall, Ernie Parkes, Cam Seagram
1940	Manitoba	Howard Wood, Ernie Pollard, Howard Wood Jr., Roy Enman
1941	Alberta	Howard Palmer, Jack Lebeau, Art Gooder, Clare Webb
1942	Manitoba	Ken Watson, Grant Watson, Charlie Scrymgeour, Jim Grant
1946	Alberta	Billy Rose, Bart Swelin, Austin Smith, George Crooks
1947	Manitoba	Jimmy Welsh, Alex Welsh, Jack Reid, Harry Monk
1948	British Columbia	Frenchy D'Amour, Bob McGhie, Fred Wendell, Jim Mark
1949	Manitoba	Ken Watson, Grant Watson, Lyle Dyker, Charles Read
1950	Northern Ontario	Tom Ramsay, Len Williamson, Bill Weston, Bill Kenny
1951	Nova Scotia	Don Oyler, George Hanson, Fred Dyke, Wally Knock
1952	Manitoba	Billy Walsh, Al Langlois, Andy McWilliams, John Watson
1953	Manitoba	Al Gowanlock, Jim Williams, Art Pollon, Russ Jackman
1954	Alberta	Matt Baldwin, Glen Gray, Pete Ferry, Jim Collins
1955	Saskatchewan	Garnet Campbell, Don Campbell, Glen Campbell, Lloyd Campbell
1956	Manitoba	Billy Walsh, Al Langlois, Cy White, Andy McWilliams
1957	Alberta	Matt Baldwin, Gordon Haynes, Art Kleinmeyer, Bill Price
1958	Alberta	Matt Baldwin, Jack Geddes, Gordon Haynes, Bill Price
1959	Saskatchewan	Ernie Richardson, Arnold Richardson, Sam Richardson, Wes Richardson
1960	Saskatchewan	Ernie Richardson, Arnold Richardson, Sam Richardson, Wes Richardson
1961	Alberta	Hec Gervais, Ron Anton, Ray Werner, Wally Ursuliak
1962	Saskatchewan	Ernie Richardson, Arnold Richardson, Sam Richardson, Wes Richardson
1963	Saskatchewan	Ernie Richardson, Arnold Richardson, Sam Richardson, Mel Perry
1964	British Columbia	Lyall Dagg, Leo Hebert, Fred Britton, Barry Naimark
1965	Manitoba	Terry Braunstein, Don Duguid, Ron Braunstein, Ray Turnbull
1966	Alberta	Ron Northcott, George Fink, Bernie Sparkes, Fred Storey
1967	Ontario	Alf Phillips Jr., John Ross, Ron Manning, Keith Reilly
1968	Alberta	Ron Northcott, Jim Shields, Bernie Sparkes, Fred Storey
1969	Alberta	Ron Northcott, Dave Gerlach, Bernie Sparkes, Fred Storey
1970	Manitoba	Don Duguid, Rod Hunter, Jim Pettapiece, Bryan Wood
1971	Manitoba	Don Duguid, Rod Hunter, Jim Pettapiece, Bryan Wood
1972	Manitoba	Orest Meleschuk, Dave Romano, John Hanesiak, Pat Hailley
1973	Saskatchewan	Harvey Mazinke, Bill Martin, George Achtymichuk, Dan Klippenstein
1974	Alberta	Hec Gervais, Ron Anton, Warren Hansen, Darrel Sutton
1975	Northern Ontario	Bill Tetley, Rick Lang, Bill Hodgson, Peter Hnatiew
1976	Newfoundland	Jack MacDuff, Toby McDonald, Doug Hudson, Ken Templeton

Canadian Men's Champions – cont'd

1977	Quebec	Jim Ursel, Art Lobel, Don Aitken, Brian Ross
1978	Alberta	Ed Lukowich, Mike Chernoff, Dale Johnston, Ron Schindle
1979	Manitoba	Barry Fry, Bill Carey, Gord Sparkes, Bryan Wood

Labatt Brier Champions

1980	Saskatchewan	Rick Folk, Ron Mills, Tom Wilson, Jim Wilson
1981	Manitoba	Kerry Burtnyk, Mark Olson, Jim Spencer, Ron Kammerlock
1982	Northern Ontario	Al Hackner, Rick Lang, Bob Nicol, Bruce Kennedy
1983	Ontario	Ed Werenich, Paul Savage, John Kawaja, Neil Harrison
1984	Manitoba	Mike Riley, Brian Toews, John Helston, Russ Wookey
1985	Northern Ontario	Al Hackner, Rick Lang, Ian Tetley, Pat Perroud
1986	Alberta	Ed Lukowich, John Ferguson, Neil Houston, Brent Syme
1987	Ontario	Russ Howard, Glenn Howard, Tim Belcourt, Ken Carstairs
1988	Alberta	Pat Ryan, Randy Ferbey, Don Walchuk, Don McKenzie
1989	Alberta	Pat Ryan, Randy Ferbey, Don Walchuk, Don McKenzie

Canadian Ladies' Champions

1961	Saskatchewan	Joyce McKee, Sylvia Fedoruk, Barbara MacNevin, Rosa McFee
1962	British Columbia	Ina Hansen, Ada Callas, Isabel Leith, May Shaw
1963	New Brunswick	Mabel DeWare, Harriet Strattan, Forbis Stevenson, Marjorie Fraser
1964	British Columbia	Ina Hansen, Ada Calles, Isabel Leith, May Shaw
1965	Manitoba	Peggy Casselman, Val Taylor, Pat MacDonald, Pat Scott
1966	Alberta	Gale Lee, Hazel Jamieson, Sharon Harrington, June Coyle
1967	Manitoba	Betty Duguid, Joan Ingram, Laurie Bradawaski, Dot Rose
1968	Alberta	Hazel Jamieson, Gale Lee, Jackie Spencer, June Coyle
1969	Saskatchewan	Joyce McKee, Vera Pezer, Lenore Morrison, Jennifer Falk
1970	Saskatchewan	Dorenda Schoenhals, Cheryl Stirton, Linda Burnham, Joan Anderson
1971	Saskatchewan	Vera Pezer, Sheila Rowan, Joyce McKee, Lenore Morrison
1972	Saskatchewan	Vera Pezer, Sheila Rowan, Joyce McKee, Lenore Morrison
1973	Saskatchewan	Vera Pezer, Sheila Rowan, Joyce McKee, Lenore Morrison
1974	Saskatchewan	Emily Farnham, Linda Saunders, Pat McBeth, Donna Collins
1975	Quebec	Lee Tobin, Marilyn McNeil, Michelle Garneau, Laurie Ross
1976	British Columbia	Lindsay Davie, Dawn Knowles, Robin Klasen, Lorraine Bowles
1977	Alberta	Myrna McQuarrie, Rita Tarvana, Barb Davis, Jane Rempel
1978	Manitoba	Cathy Pidzarko, Chris Pidzarko, Iris Armstrong, Patti Vande
1979	British Columbia	Lindsay Sparkes, Dawn Knowles, Robin Wilson, Lorraine Bowles
1980	Saskatchewan	Marj Mitchell, Nancy Kerr, Shirley McKendry, Wendy Leach
1981	Alberta	Susan Seitz, Judy Erickson, Myrna McKay, Betty McCracken
1982	Nova Scotia	Colleen Jones, Kay Smith, Monica Jones, Barbara Jones-Gordon
1983	Nova Scotia	Penny LaRocque, Sharon Horne, Cathy Caudle, Pam Sanford
1984	Manitoba	Connie Laliberte, Chris More, Corrine Peters, Janet Arnott
1985	British Columbia	Linda Moore, Lindsay Sparkes, Debbie Jones, Laurie Carney
1986	Ontario	Marilyn Darte, Kathy McEdwards, Chris Jurgenson, Jan Augustyn
1987	British Columbia	Pat Sanders, Georgina Hawkes, Louise Herlinveaux, Deb Massullo
1988	Northern Ontario	Heather Houston, Lorraine Lang, Diane Adams, Tracy Kennedy
1989	Team Canada	Heather Houston, Lorraine Lang, Diane Adams, Tracy Kennedy

Canadian Senior Men's Champions

Seagram Stone Champions

1965	Manitoba	Leo Johnson, Marno Frederickson, Fred Smith, Cliff Wise
1966	Ontario	Jim Johnston, Tom Rosborough, Joe Todd, Ed Waller
1967	New Brunswick	Jim Murphy, Harry Farrell, Don Beatteay, Walter Biddiscombe
1968	Saskatchewan	Don Wilson, Carson Tufts, Ivan McMillan, Reuben Lowe
1969	Ontario	Alfie Phillips, George Cowan, Sandy McTavish, Jack Young
1970	British Columbia	Don MacRae, Gene Koster, Bev Smiley, Doc Howden
1971	Prince Edward Island	Wen MacDonald, John Squarebriggs, Doug George, Dan O'Rourke
1972	Quebec	Ken Weldon, Ben McCormick, Bob Hubbard, Larry Elliott
1973	Manitoba	Bill McTavish, Bunt McLean, John McLean, Harry Sulkers
1974	British Columbia	George Beaudry, Buzz McGibney, Tom Clark, Harvey McKay

C.C.A. Seniors Champions

1975	Prince Edward Island	Wen MacDonald, John Squarebriggs, Irvine MacKinnon, Don Hutchison
1976	Prince Edward Island	Wen MacDonald, John Squarebriggs, Irvine MacKinnon, Don Hutchison
1977	Saskatchewan	Morrie Thompson, Bert Harbottle, Archie Bartley, Mac McKee
1978	Saskatchewan	Art Knutson, Ernie Vaughan, Gay Knutson, Elmer Knutson
1979	Alberta	Cliff Forry, John Wolfe, Fred Kalicum, Ray Wellman
1980	Saskatchewan	Terry McGeary, Don Berglind, Hillis Thompson, Clare Ramsay
1981	Quebec	Jim Wilson, Garth Ruiter, George Brown, Bert Skitt
1982	Manitoba	Lloyd Gunnlaugson, Toru Suzuki, Albert Olson, Elgin Christianson
1983	Manitoba	Lloyd Gunnlaugson, Toru Suzuki, Albert Olson, Dennis Reid
1984	Manitoba	Lloyd Gunnlaugson, Toru Suzuki, Albert Olson, Elgin Christianson
1985	Saskatchewan	Frank Scheirich, Joe Golumbia, Wally Yuzdepski, Alex Wassien
1986	Ontario	Earle Hushagen, Joe Gurowka, Art Lobel, Bert Baragan

Canadian Senior Men's Champions – cont'd

1987	Manitoba	Norm Houck, Henry Kroeger, Sam Doherty, Doug McCartney
1988	Alberta	Bill Clark, Cy Little, Murray MacDonald, John Mayer
1989	Ontario	Jim Sharples, Art Lobel, Joe Gurowka, Peter Warren

Canadian Senior Ladies' Champions

1973	British Columbia	Ada Calles, Ina Hansen, Mae Shaw, Barbara Weir
1974	British Columbia	Flora Martin, Edna Messum, Doreen Baker, Betty Stubbs
1975	British Columbia	Flora Martin, Edna Messum, Doreen Baker, Betty Stubbs
1976	Alberta	Hadie Manley, Bernie Durward, Anna Kasting, Gladys Baptist
1977	British Columbia	Vi Tapella, Rose Neratini, Doris Driesche, Mary Lee Bacchus
1978	Alberta	Hadie Manley, Bernie Durward, Dee McIntyre, Anna Kasting
1979	British Columbia	Flora Martin, Elsie Humphrey, Verle McKeown, Edna Messum
1980	British Columbia	Flora Martin, Elsie Humphrey, Verle McKeown, Edna Messum
1981	Alberta	Bea Mayer, Eileen Cyr, Leah Nate, Alice Vejprava
1982	Nova Scotia	Verda Kempton, Lucille Hamm, Molly Pirie, Lois Smith
1983	Manitoba	Mabel Mitchell, Mary Adams, Mildred Murray, June Clark
1984	Saskatchewan	Ev Krahn, Twyla Widdifield, Shirley Little, June Kaufman
1985	Saskatchewan	Ev Krahn, Twyla Widdifield, Shirley Little, June Kaufman
1986	Saskatchewan	Ev Krahn, Twyla Widdifield, Shirley Little, June Kaufman
1987	Nova Scotia	Verda Kempton, Marita Morrow, Joan Mason, Molly Pirie
1988	Ontario	Phyllis Nielsen, Barbara Baird, Geraldine Barton, Mary Ellen McGugan
1989	Saskatchewan	Emily Farnham, Mary Todarchuk, Emily Heidt, Arlik Ellsworth

Bibliography

The Calgary Curling Club. *Calgary Curling Club 1888-1988 A Roaring Century.* Calgary: Calgary Curling Club, 1988.

Cowan, Bob. *Curling and the Siver Broom.* Glasgow: Richard Drew Publishing, 1985.

Creelman, W.A. *Curling Past and Present.* Toronto: McClelland & Stewart, 1950.

Maxwell, Doug, and Friends. *The First Fifty.* Toronto: Maxcurl Publications, 1980.

Murray, W.H. *The Curling Companion.* Toronto: Collins, 1982.

Richardson, Ernie, et al. *Curling.* New York: David McKay Co., 1963.

The Royal Caledonian Curling Club. *Annual 1987-88.* Edinburgh: Royal Caledonian Curling Club, 1988.

The Royal Montreal Curling Club. *One Hundred and Fifty Years of Curling (1807-1957).* Montreal: Privately printed, 1957.

Smith, David B. *Curling: an Illustrated History.* Edinburgh: John Donald Publishers, 1981.

Watson, Ken. *Ken Watson on Curling.* Toronto: Copp Clark, 1950.

Welsh, Robin. *Beginner's Guide to Curling.* London: Pelham Books, 1969.
International Guide to Curling. London: Pelham Books, 1985.

Magazines, Newspapers, Manuals

Canadian Curling Association. *Championship Hosting Manual,* 1988.

Canadian Curling Association. *1988-89 Curling Fact Book.* Gloucester, Ont.: National Office of Curling, 1989.

Corcoran, Linda. *Little Rock Curling.* Willowdale, Ont.: Ontario Curling Federation, 1988.

Dilschneider, Donna, ed. *Ontario Curling Report.* Toronto: Peter Birchard, et al.

Hansen, Warren, ed. *Curling Canada.* Toronto: National All-Sports Promotions.

Kitchener-Waterloo 1986 Labatt Brier Souvenir Program.

Labatt's National Curling Trials Souvenir Program, 1987.

Maxwell, Doug, ed. *Canadian Curling News.* Toronto: Doug Maxwell.

Saskatoon 1989 Labatt Brier Souvenir Program.

Schuchard, Rick, ed. *Northern Curling Review.* Edmonton, Alta.: Riegel Publications Ltd.

Credits

Hugh Allan page 48; Athlete Information Bureau and Canadian Olympic Association pages 96, 101 (bottom); Austrian National Tourist Office pages 18 (bottom), 87; Frank Baratta page 62; Ron Burgess (Scottish Daily Express) pages 38-39; Michael Burns pages 56, 89, 108, 109 (bottom), 110, 111, 113, 114, 115, 116, 122, 123, 125, 128 (top), 134; Buxton Museum and Art Gallery pages 64, 65; Calgary Curling Club page 47; Canadian Curling Association page 50; Canapress Photo Service page 79; Dave Chidley pages 24, 120-121, 147 (bottom), 148 (bottom); Sir John Clerk of Penicuik pages 36-37; Bob Cowan pages 20 (left), 31 (bottom); The Curling Hall of Fame and Museum of Canada page 126; Svein E. Furulund/A-FOTO pages 77, 99, 100 (top); German National Tourist Office page 18 (top); Enzo Giuliano pages 20 (right), 41, 43; Warren Hansen pages 57 (top), 121; Dennis Hernus page 63 (bottom); R. Homberger (Arosa) pages 82-83, 85; Axel Kamp (Swedish Curling Association) pages 70, 71, 72, 73; Hiroshi Kobayashi pages 30, 92, 93, 94, 105, 107; Kunsthistorisches Museum (Vienna) pages 11, 12; Labatt's (Michael Burns) pages 27, 52 (bottom), 54, 58 (bottom), 59 (bottom), 61 (left), 128 (bottom), 129, 130, 131, 132 (center), 136, 137 (bottom), 138, 139 (top), 142 (top), 143, 145, 146, 149, 150; Allan Leishman page 140 (top); Hans T. Lokken pages 74-75; Doug Maxwell pages 55, 137 (diagram); Greg Morrison pages 58 (top), 127, 132 (top and bottom); Musées royaux des Beaux-Arts de Belgique (Brussels) pages 14-15; National Archives of Canada pages 40, 42 (top), 44, 45, 46, 49; National Gallery of Scotland pages 4-5; Notman Photographic Archives, McCord Museum of Canadian History pages 42 (bottom), 118-19; Bill Paulson pages 66-67; Michael Pugh page 100 (bottom); Rijksmuseum (Amsterdam) page 17; Royal Caledonian Curling Club pages 28-29, 32, 33 (Rules); Ernst Schudel pages 80, 84 (top); Scottish Curling Museum Trust pages 31, 117; David B. Smith page 95; Swiss National Tourist Office page 84 (bottom); VG (Norway) pages 103, 106, 140-41; Brad Watson pages 120 (top), 133, 139 (bottom), 147 (top), 148 (top); Robin Welsh of Edinburgh, Editor, "The Scottish Curler" pages 53, 63 (top: photo by Mr. Cowper), 97 (bottom); Page 52 (top): Privately owned.

Acknowledgements

The authors and editors wish to thank the following for their contribution to this book:

Doug Maxwell

David B. Smith

Robin Welsh

Bob Cowan

Warren Hansen

Bo Bakke

Axel Kamp

Håkan Sundström

Perthi Sipilainen

Leif Grönlund

M.L.Birch

Peter von Gunten

Ernst Schudel

Raymond Ducroz

Ivo Lorenzi

Tetsuo Tanaka

Hiroshi Kobayashi

M.P. Wentworth

Ann Stone

Mrs. Elizabeth Patterson-Brown

John M.L. Brown

Allan Leishman

Malcolm Turner

Canadian Curling Association

Labatt Breweries of Canada

Royal Caledonian Curling Club

Canadian Branch of Royal Caledonian

U.S. Curling Association

International Curling Federation

Quebec Curling Federation

Royal Montreal Curling Club

Calgary Curling Club

Glenmore Curling Club

Lachine Curling Club

A-High Tech Photography (Albert Wong)